"A most timely, perceptive, and life-giving book. I heartily recommend *Fanning the Flame* as a very well written, practical, biblical, and anointed call to spiritual revitalization and health. Terri Clark puts forward an incredibly important message to all who desire an ongoing, vital relationship with Christ and long-term fruitfulness in the kingdom of God."

—**Tim McKitrick, DMin,** Executive Director, World Ministry Fellowship

"Terri has written a must-read for anyone seeking to reignite the fire in their walk with God. Her personal experiences reflect a struggle that most Christians go through in their relationship with Christ. This book is a great guide on how to reignite that fire and bring the spark in our Christian walk."

—**Monique Mubiru,** Founder & Director, Ray of Hope Ministries, Uganda

"What happens when we get routine or even forget to talk, really talk, to God? Our Christian lives are crippled with lack of power—lack of meaning. Terri Clark walks us through events in her life when she struggled, and how God showed her the way back. You'll laugh and you will cry at the stories of God's grace, mercy, and love. *Fanning the Flame* is now on my once-a-year reading list!"

—**Phil Burks,** CEO, The Genesis Group, Tyler, TX
(global software company)

"What a gift to be given! Terri Clark has written a wonderful guide to help us make the journey back both to God and to who we are. She tells us in many ways how to fan the flames in order for our embers to burn again. Take heart. There *is* a way back into the fold!"

—**Polly Mitchell Giles,** actress, vocalist, precision/stunt driver
(*Fast 7* and *Need for Speed*)

"Terri has done it again! *Fanning the Flame* is relevant for busy, over-committed people like me. Her easy-to-follow storytelling kept my interest and attention. Her 'tell it like it is' truth covered with personal confessions makes it easy to embrace. This is a busy Christian's must-read."

—**Mickey Gates,** Arkansas State Representative

# Fanning the Flame

# Fanning the Flame

## Reigniting Your Faith in God

# TERRI CLARK

# LEAFWOOD
P U B L I S H E R S
*an imprint of Abilene Christian University Press*

# FANNING THE FLAME
*Reigniting Your Faith in God*

## LEAFWOOD
### P U B L I S H E R S
*an imprint of Abilene Christian University Press*

Copyright © 2017 by Terri Clark

ISBN 978-0-89112-587-7  |  LCCN 2017040001

Printed in the United States of America

Published in association with the Hartline Literary Agency, 123 Queenston Drive, Pittsburgh, PA 15235.

LIBRARY OF CONGRESS CATALOGING-IN-PUBLICATION DATA
Names: Clark, Terri, 1954- author.
Title: Fanning the flame : reigniting your faith in God / Terri Clark.
Description: Abilene, Texas : Leafwood Publishers, 2017.
Identifiers: LCCN 2017040001 | ISBN 9780891125877 (pbk.)
Subjects: LCSH: Christian life.
Classification: LCC BV4501.3 .C5243 2017 | DDC 248.4—dc23
LC record available at https://lccn.loc.gov/ 2017040001

Cover design by ThinkPen Design, LLC | Interior text design by Sandy Armstrong, Strong Design

Leafwood Publishers is an imprint of Abilene Christian University Press
ACU Box 29138, Abilene, Texas 79699

1-877-816-4455 | www.leafwoodpublishers.com

17 18 19 20 21 22 / 7 6 5 4 3 2 1

*Now we see but a dim reflection as in a mirror;*
*then we shall see face to face.*
*Now I know in part; then I shall know fully,*
*even as I am fully known.*
—1 Corinthians 13:12 BSB

I would like to dedicate this book to my son, Jeremy,
who is now seeing Jesus face to face.

# Contents

# Acknowledgments

Writing a book is no easy task, especially when you're a wife, mother, and grandmother in a family of twenty-three. It's especially challenging when you also have a ministry to run, so the publication of this book never could have happened without the help of everyone close to me. Without getting too mushy, I first want to acknowledge and thank my amazing husband, Harvey Clark, for his rock-solid support in this project. Without him pushing me, praying for me, and prodding me up the hill to my camper to write, I might never have gotten past the first page. Harvey, you're my hero!

I am grateful for each person in my huge family for their support and understanding during the times I was sequestered and stressed. Y'all are the best! I'm especially grateful to Sara for the way she took charge so I could write—planning meals, grocery shopping, and putting everything on a calendar so I wouldn't have to think about it. Who does that? You're an amazing daughter!

I especially want to thank our dear friend, Dale, a retired pastor and Can-Am Spyder riding buddy. Your stories, comments, and especially your prayers were invaluable—it was great having a pastor to bounce my thoughts and ideas off of.

To my Ugandan twin, Monique Mubiru, and our Armor Bearers, the women both in Uganda and the United States who have committed themselves to pray daily for our ministries: thank you for standing with me as I've labored on this book. To Tracy, my right-hand woman, I'm thankful for your capable handling of all the ministry details. And of course, my best friend and ministry buddy, Nancy. Thank you for coaching me, praying for me, and being my cheerleader. I love you dearly. I am grateful to everyone who took the time to pray over this book—there are too many to list, but God knows your name. May the smoldering embers of faith in every person who reads this book be fanned into a blazing flame as a result of your faithful intercession.

# Flickering Flames

"For this reason I remind you to fan into flame
the gift of God, which is in you . . ."

—2 Timothy 1:6 ESV

**As I sit here cradling** a cup of tea in front of the fireplace, I can't help but think back to a mission trip I took to a nation in Southeast Asia.

I traveled with a team of amazing women to speak and minister at a retreat for English-speaking missionaries. Counting it a privilege and honor to serve these ladies and to bring *them* an encouraging word, I hoped, and even expected, to glean a little spiritual insight for myself from these unsung heroes.

But after only a few conversations, it hit me that many of these women were on the verge of burnout. Their fires that once burned brightly for Jesus had diminished to smoldering wicks and flickering flames. Discouraged and tired, some were even ready to pack up and go home.

These women weren't novices; they were women of the Word. Having calculated the cost of mission life, they *chose* to trade a comfortable life in their home countries—the United States,

13

United Kingdom, Australia, Canada, and so on—for a much harder life in a nation that was not only difficult for them culturally, but also closed to the gospel. Many had families with small children who had never met their grandparents back home. Some of their children were older and had spent most of their adult lives there. All of these missionaries started out zealously in love with Jesus, so how did they get to that place of burnout spiritually?

Watching the crackling embers of the fire burn down, my mind raced to friends I've known over the course of my forty-year walk with God who have thrown in their faith towels and chosen to live a secular life in the world. These men and women had been committed to Jesus; they were serving him and knew his Word. I saw their faces and remembered great times of fellowship and worship, even serious conversations about faith and Christian values.

Where are they now? A few are walking in blatant sin, but many are just living their lives apart from God. None of these friends attend church. The focus of their lives is on work, family, friends, and activities—and while there's nothing wrong with those things, it seems God and faith have been forgotten. And to be perfectly honest, my toes have dangled dangerously over the edge of this very same pit more than I care to admit.

Seeing all these faces in my mind, I can't help but ask the Lord, "How does that happen?" Some were pastors and teachers, and many were good friends who made up the core of their churches. They were ordinary people who loved God—moms, dads, businesspeople, and leaders.

I refilled my cup of tea, thinking about my own ministry and walk with the Lord. I wonder, what will keep the light of my own lamp from burning out? How do I fan the flames and reignite *my* spiritual fire? In a time of increasing wickedness in the world and with the return of Christ drawing near, I can't help but examine my own spiritual health and walk with God. Will I be ready when the trumpet is sounded?

If burnout could happen to these missionaries in Southeast Asia and to so many of my friends in the faith, it could happen to me. Just think about all the big-name Christian leaders who have fallen into sin. Obviously, no one is exempt.

I know and love the Scriptures. I've gained insight and understanding while studying and applying God's Word to my life and helping others apply it to theirs. But I'm not where I want to be, nor where I think I should be after studying the Word and professing Christ for more than forty years. So I ask: Where have I missed the mark? When did my distance from God begin?

## Where Distance Begins

For many believers in Christ who take their faith seriously, commitment to Jesus is more than Sunday morning church—it is a way of life. We embrace a Christ-centered life, and that affects our values, including every decision we make, how we raise our children, the friends we keep, books we read, movies we watch, music we listen to, people we vote for, and virtually every other aspect of daily living.

All those things are well and good, but are they enough? Is it enough to just believe in and talk about Jesus under the increasing pressures of the world we live in? When I look at newspaper headlines, turn on the television, read books, or surf around on the Internet, it's obvious—our nation is moving away from God at an alarming rate.

Signs of the times are all around. Sin is not only in our faces—it's actually being celebrated. It's not just out in the alleyways and dark corners of the world, either. The very same sin is in the church, our schools, and yes, even our homes.

The more we see it, the more we overlook it; and the more we overlook, the less we love. Judgment or indifference replaces compassion and love. We are still out there doing the work of the Lord, but the love and compassion we once had for the lost is diminishing. This, of course, doesn't just affect our relationships with other people—it also affects our relationship with God.

I'm not condemning or judging. I'm just pointing out that distance from God happens when we move away from God—not the other way around. He is calling his people to not just behave like good Christians, but also to come back to him with their whole heart—to worship him with humility and reverence, and to have attentive ears to hear what the Spirit is saying.

He wants us to read his Word, but also to consume it, obey it, and allow it to transform us into his image. The Lord wants to use us to draw others to him by our answering his call to share the gospel and serve others—whether by preaching, praying, working, or just loving the unlovely. God is calling his people back and asking them to once again make a living sacrifice of their whole hearts.

## Divided Hearts

When I gave my life to Jesus, I gave him my whole heart. I was sold-out, hook, line, and sinker—and I still am, forty years later. But life happens, and even if we are sold-out Christians, our hearts do become divided.

I think we can sense a distance from God happening when our busy lives pull us in several directions. We know we need to draw closer to God, so we resolve to pray and read our Bibles more, and to do more to get back to where we think we need to be spiritually.

But our human nature tends to look at those things as just adding something else to an already full plate, so we put them off.

It's sort of like starting a diet—I'll start as soon as the holidays have passed. Or beginning an exercise routine—I'll start walking when the weather cools down. In reality, we don't always have the option to change the circumstances we live in to accommodate what our hearts want to do. Life just happens. The general busyness of life can consume the lion's share of our time, no matter who we are or where we live.

Pastors will continue to live in fish bowls, be wakened by 3:00 A.M. phone calls, and be expected to have all the answers. Sleep-deprived young mothers will continue to get up at all hours of the night with their babies. The pressures of life will continue to be magnified for single parents. Truck drivers will spend more time away from their families than they would like. Dads will come home from a hard day's work and wrestle with the kids on the floor even though every muscle in their body is crying out for the couch. Shift workers will get their days and nights confused. Working mothers will still have to fix dinner for their hungry families at the end of a long day. Students will be overloaded with papers to write, and teachers will still have to stay up late grading these papers. You get the idea—life just happens.

The busyness of life, along with our call to serve others, will likely continue to put demands on our time and energy, squeezing time with God down to little or nothing. As much as our spirit desires to carve out that time for him, our flesh is weak.

When we spend less time in fellowship with God and less time drawing from his wisdom, strength, and grace, we naturally begin to lean on our own perceived wisdom, strength, and abilities to work, live life, and try to save the world.

## Living on Fast Food

If you're like me and most other believers, time gets away from you, and before you realize it, your oil is burned down and you find yourself running on spiritual fumes. Instead of refueling, we just keep on going, with every intention of taking time out to spend with God—this is, of course, on our list of things to do.

We get into the habit of praying on the go, listening to messages on the radio while we drive, or skimming nuggets from an e-book while waiting for our next appointment, but we run out of day before we've had the time to quiet our minds and hearts to really listen to what the Holy Spirit wants to reveal to us in his Word or speak to us in prayer.

It's kind of like living on fast food, grabbing a bite here and there as we speed from one activity to the next. While the food quiets our growling stomachs, it isn't healthy. Over time, our bodies begin to rebel by storing up fat, and we don't quite have the energy level we once had to keep up with the demands of our busy lives.

Our spirit is just like our body—it craves "real food," a balanced diet of home-cooked meals. God knows this, and he has a table set for us, filled with delicious foods prepared just the way we love them. But we are just too busy to sit down and dine with him. Fast food becomes our spiritual preference because it doesn't require as much of our time and focus. And if we are honest, it keeps us from addressing the guilt we heap upon ourselves for allowing our hearts to drift so far from him while living the "Christian life." A diet of stressful demands on our time and energies, in combination with not availing ourselves to God to replenish our oil supply, is spiritually depleting, leaving us open and vulnerable for the enemy to come rushing in.

We are a little like lobsters slowly cooking in a boiling pot, becoming so comfortable with the sin around us that it's hard to detect the effect it's having on us as believers until it's too late. For most of us, we don't even realize we are moving away until we find ourselves vulnerably standing smack-dab in the middle of a difficult situation. Someone offends us, a job is lost, needs pile up in our family or ministry work, the doctor gives us a bad report, the electricity is shut off . . . fill in your own blanks—we all have them.

Of course, we cry out to God for help, because that's what Christians do, right? But then, because we are spiritually depleted, we find ourselves reacting in the flesh. Instead of responding with grace and compassion, we get angry or hurt—talking about it to anyone who will listen, jumping on Facebook to throw stones, or just giving up and shutting down. And depending on how low our flame is burning, we begin to relive our past—abuses, betrayals, and anything else Satan can remind us of—causing us to react even more from the flesh to our current circumstances and to other people.

## Stirring Up the Embers

With my teacup now empty, the fire in the fireplace has settled into an orange glow. Left alone, it will eventually grow cold. The last log is partially burnt and smoldering, and if I don't act, the flame might die.

The life of the Holy Spirit within us is like that—even if that fire has dwindled to smoldering embers, it still has life, and those coals have the potential to become a blazing fire again. It just needs another log to be tossed on it for fuel and a little fanning to get the flame going.

I don't know about you, but I want to feel that fire. I want to know its warmth and power in my life. I want to have an expectant zeal for God again, with a heart that looks like his, full of compassion and grace. The Spirit of Christ *is* in us. We *can* throw on another log and stoke up our smoldering embers.

If you've picked up this book, I assume those spiritual embers are still alive in you and that you're ready to fan them back into a flame. The good news is this: we don't have to do it alone. I love that about God. Not only is he the fire within us, he's also the one who provides the fuel and motivates us to stoke up the embers—then his Spirit blows on them so we can burn again. God is for us! And if God is for us, who can be against us?

# Chapter 1

# Finding Our Way Back

"Seek the LORD and His strength; Seek His face continually."
—Psalms 105:4 NASB

**Just the mere suggestion that** we might want to find our way back to God is kind of misleading because, in all sincerity, we haven't really left him. We still love God and have a heart to serve him. For the sake of clarity, I want to point out that it's the closeness and intimacy with our Lord Jesus that makes us passionate about living for and serving him—that's what we hope to regain.

Let's begin this pilgrimage by laying aside our guilt trips and self-condemnation. God doesn't want to douse your smoldering wick with condemnation or judgment. You are, and always will be, his favorite son or daughter. He is running toward you to bless and encourage you, just as the father of the prodigal son did when his boy came to his senses and decided to come home. You may not have been out in the world squandering wealth or eating pig slop, or maybe you have! Either way, God will always run to you with the same enthusiasm and meet your desire to find your way back to his heart. Like he said to the prodigal's brother, "Look, dear son . . .

21

you and I are very close, and everything I have is yours. But it is right to celebrate. For he is your brother; and he was dead and has come back to life! He was lost and is found!" (Luke 15:31–32 TLB).

God is for us. God is for YOU (Rom. 8:31). And with God on our side, our flickering flames can and will blaze again.

## Fanning the Flame

The fire is there, but it needs to be fanned. That's what the apostle Paul told Timothy, his young son in the faith: "fan into flame the gift of God, which is in you . . . " (2 Tim. 1:6 ESV). In this second letter to Timothy, Paul seemed to have detected a frustration or weariness. He addressed several issues that may have contributed to the young pastor's flickering flame.

Timothy, like us, had a lot on his plate, and was probably feeling overwhelmed and possibly a little burned out. Because Paul had a history with this young man's family, he knew Timothy's story. So he started out Timothy's letter of encouragement by looking back, telling his protégé that he remembered the genuine faith that started in his mom and grandmother, and how he was convinced this faith was in Timothy as well.

Throughout the Old Testament, God instructed his people to look back and remember. He even had them set up memorial stones, instruct their children about the meaning of these memorials, and keep the feasts, so in looking back, they'd always remember God's mighty works and the unique relationship he has with his people.

It never hurts us to look back to remind ourselves of God's redeeming grace, especially if we've been a believer for a while. This is particularly important for those of us whose lives are busy and who feel like we've been in a spiritual rut. We need memorial stones to remind us of who God is and what he has done in our lives. These memorial stones mark spots in our lives—real times and places where significant events happened between us and God. One of my own memorial stones is an old piece of furniture—an old, gray chair.

## The Old, Gray Chair

Back in the 1970s, when I was a brand-new Christian, I lived in an upstairs apartment in Pennsylvania. Our living room was furnished with an old, gray, second-hand sofa and chair set from the 1950s—the kind that had rough nylon texture.

Every night after putting my two-year-old son to bed, I got down on my knees in front of this old, gray chair in the corner of my living room and talked to God—about everything. Our conversations sometimes went late into the night. I read my Bible every day like it was a best-selling novel. Except, I knew this book wasn't fiction. If the Bible said it, I believed it! And since God doesn't change, I was confident he would do for me what he did for the people in the Bible. God responded to the prayers of faith whispered in front of that old, gray chair.

Back in those "beans and rice days," there were times when my cupboards were bare. On my knees, with my head burrowed into the rough gray nylon of the old, gray chair, I reminded God of a place in the Bible where he said his children would not have to beg for bread. By the time I got up to go to bed, I fully expected God to meet my need.

The next morning, there they were—three bags of groceries on my doorstep. I never knew who left them. It could have been someone from my church or a visiting angel, I don't know. But you can believe me when I tell you that it was God who got all the glory and thanks.

One frigid winter, while snuggled down in my old, gray chair with a warm blanket and my Bible, the story of the widow whose oil was multiplied came alive to me (2 Kings 4:1–7). We still had about a week to go before payday, but hardly any food in the house. Knowing God doesn't show favoritism (Rom. 2:11 BSB), I took my position in front of the old, gray chair on my knees and asked him to stretch our food, just like he did for that widow, so I could make meals for my family until the next paycheck.

About all I had left in the kitchen was a small box of instant rice. The box was made with a spout on the side to pour rice out as needed, so I couldn't actually see inside. By shaking it, I knew the box was nearly empty, with probably less than an inch of rice on the bottom. But that little bit of rice kept pouring out. Our family ate from that near-empty box all week long.

Now, I'm not saying that God always answered my prayers in miraculous ways, nor am I saying he gave me everything I asked for. Sometimes he said no. But there was something special about our relationship that caused me to truly know he loved me, regardless of whether I got what I prayed for. I loved God, and just wanted to be with him and live my life for him.

Looking back at my "memorial stone" (my old, gray chair), it really wasn't that old, gray chair—it was the presence of God and the intimate friendship I had with him whenever I spent time in that special place.

## Practicing His Presence

Looking back and remembering "what used to be," of course, isn't enough to get the fire going again, but it can motivate us to action—the action of practicing his presence. This is something we can do, no matter what kind of life we might have swirling around us.

The idea of practicing the presence of God comes from a seventeenth-century monk named Brother Lawrence, who lived in a French monastery in the 1600s. Through letters and conversations, Brother Lawrence simply and beautifully explained how to continually walk with God—not from the head, but from the heart. After his death in 1691, these letters and conversations were published in a pamphlet titled *The Practice of the Presence of God*.

Brother Lawrence's direct approach to living in God's presence is as practical today as it was three hundred years ago. You don't have to be a monk to live continually in God's presence; in fact, people with busy lives like us can find freedom in following Brother Lawrence's example.

What did this old monk do that was so unique and special to stay in God's presence? It's really very simple—aware that God is always with us, Brother Lawrence acknowledged him in all he did, all the time. That's it. Rather than focusing on setting aside a time to pray over needs, he made a habit of continually conversing with God throughout each day, always desiring to honor the Lord in his actions and words. Whether he was working, going to the market, or interacting with other people, he practiced God's continual presence.

This doesn't mean you can't have that special time in front of your version of the old, gray chair, because those times are important and special and they do build us up spiritually. But as you develop a constant dialogue with God throughout the day, your spiritual oil will be continually replenished. And when you do have time to quietly sit with the Lord, your fellowship with him will be that much sweeter.

You may have heard the saying "He's so spiritually minded, he's no earthly good"—that isn't what we're talking about. Practicing the presence of God isn't living life on a cloud; on the contrary, it's living life with a fresh awareness of God's ever-present companionship in every circumstance and conversation. With God walking alongside you, you don't have to wait to talk to him about anything.

I admire people who know how to pray, those who have a natural way of communicating with God. Words just always seem to flow. When they say they'll pray about something, they do. For some, spending hours and even days before God is not uncommon. It is where they live their lives. I think King David was probably one of those people. His psalms have the fragrance of a close friendship between man and God. David didn't just ask for things; he loved God first. When he was in pain, angry, in need of help, or up against a wall, he prayed. He was expectant, and he trusted God completely.

That's what I want to experience again in my relationship with God. If you read through the psalms of David, a common thread runs through them—David was very human in his emotions, yet reverent and worshipful. David spilled his guts, but then always declared the greatness of God and how his love toward him was ever faithful and trustworthy. David praised God in the midst of his worst battles and trials. He put all his trust in God. Is it any wonder God called him a man after his own heart? (Acts 13:22).

What I don't see in these psalms is a prayer list. David prayed for the situation in front of him, but I don't see anywhere that he went down a long list of needs. I'm not saying we should throw out our prayer lists, but I do think we sometimes get overwhelmed before we even get the first few items or people checked off.

I have a big family. At times, I have prayed by going down the list for every family member by name and need. But by the time I get down to the sixth or seventh grandchild, I feel overwhelmed by all the other people I want to pray for, not to mention ministry needs and my own personal struggles. In this way, prayer and time with God can become a chore, rather than a place of refuge and peace as it should be.

Practicing God's presence isn't just praying down a list. It entails conversing with God as you take a shower, pack school lunches, pass a screaming ambulance, prepare a sermon, visit someone in the hospital, or listen to a coworker tell you about her recent breakup. Practicing the presence of God can be as simple as making yourself aware of all that is going on around you, talking to God about it, and then listening for the Holy Spirit's response.

If you're pumping gas and see the guy next to you smiling at his infant in the car seat while carefully stopping his pump at five dollars, listening to God means paying attention to the Holy Spirit's tap on your shoulder to reach into your pocket to give that guy the twenty-dollar bill you've been hanging on to. It's whispering a prayer or giving a word of encouragement to the young mother struggling to manage a fussy baby while her toddler is grabbing things off the shelves in the grocery store. It's talking over an important decision with God while you're driving down the road or peeling potatoes for dinner.

Yes, it's important to pray for needs and guidance, but you don't have to have a specific time and place to come into God's presence. Remember, you are the temple of the Holy Spirit. He is ever-present in time of need. He is always attentive to your prayers, whether spoken on your knees in front of an old, gray chair or while you're stuck in rush hour traffic.

Of course, this kind of praying-without-ceasing habit takes time to develop, especially if your oil is a little low and your wick hasn't been trimmed in a while. But there is no need to condemn yourself or give up.

According to his letters and conversations with Joseph de Beaufort (the man who first published *The Practice of the Presence of God*), even Brother Lawrence became busy and forgot to talk to God at times. When he did, he didn't put himself under condemnation. He just admitted his failings, accepted grace, and continued on. He could do this, because practicing the presence of God is also practicing the love and mercy of God.

As we begin to walk in this continuous communication with God, it will become easier to lay our burdens and struggles at Jesus's feet.

Crippled in the Thirty Years' War before he became a monk, Brother Lawrence walked with great pain and difficulty. Once, when his superior asked him to go to the city of Burgundy and bring back a provision of wine from the monastery, Brother Lawrence told God he would require his strength and help for the task.

The monk's sentiments on his assignment are recorded in his conversation with Joseph de Beaufort: "This was a challenge for him because of his lame leg and because he had no real head for business. He couldn't even get around on the boat except by dragging himself from cask to cask."[1]

How many of us, when we face unwelcome tasks, grumble or find excuses not to do them? How many of us never even think about God being right there with us, ready to provide whatever we need to get through it—even if it means doing things the hard way and dragging ourselves over a few casks?

Obviously, no one is perfect, and we are all going to mess up at times. But imagine how different our attitudes would be if we walked in continual communication with God—his mercy and grace would become second nature to us. Repentance and confessing our failings would come quickly and easily. We would be so acutely aware of God's presence, so aware that he is listening and ready to forgive us, that we would repent without suffering any separation from him.

This is what Paul was talking about in 1 Thessalonians 5:16–18 when he said, "Rejoice always, pray continually, give thanks in all circumstances; for this is God's will for you in Christ Jesus" (NIV).

Galatians 5:25 says, "If we live in the Spirit, let us also walk in the Spirit" (KJ21). That is what this is—walking it out. We know God will never leave us or forsake us, so instead of waiting for the perfect time or perfect circumstance to talk to Jesus, why not go through our days acknowledging and "practicing" his presence?

## Put Down Your Smartphone

Speaking of acknowledging someone's presence, we have a rule in our house: no smartphones or electronics at the dinner table. How many times have you been to a restaurant and observed five or six people around the table, none of whom is talking to each other because they're all either texting or otherwise absorbed in their smartphones, oblivious to their surroundings?

My husband and I noticed a family doing this one time, but with one exception. The youngest child, about eight or nine years old, didn't have a phone. Everyone at the table was so engaged in their social media conversations that no one acknowledged this boy. He just sat at the table full of people, all alone.

I think sometimes this is how God must see us. We are so occupied with our own social worlds, talking to anyone who will listen about *our* needs, *our* dreams, *our* fears, *our* wants, even *our* ministries, but never looking up to see that Jesus is right there with us, waiting for us to engage *him* in conversation about those things. Practicing the presence of God is a little like putting down our smartphones and talking to Jesus, who is sitting right there at the table with us.

### Note

[1]Robert Elmer, *Practicing God's Presence: Brother Lawrence for Today's Reader (Quiet Times for the Heart)* (Colorado Springs: NavPress, 2005), 124–25, Kindle edition.

# Chapter 2

# The Pilgrimage

"Blessed are those whose strength is in you,
   whose hearts are set on pilgrimage."

—Psalms 84:5 NIV

We are about to begin a pilgrimage. More than just taking a trip or vacation to get away for a while, a pilgrimage is a personal spiritual journey. While some pilgrimages do take the sojourner from one geographical place to another, this one will be an inward sojourn—without any physical travel at all.

I don't know what your spiritual flame looks like right now. It could be smoldering, a flicker of a flame, or perhaps a slow steady burn. Regardless of what it might look like, my prayer is that while on this Christian pilgrimage, if you are attentive and open to the Holy Spirit during each step along the way, your spiritual flame will be fanned a little more until your faith in him has been fully reignited, red hot and blazing.

But before setting out on any journey, especially this type of one, it's always a good idea to know where you want to end up and what you'll need for the road. Ask yourself where you want to be in your relationship with God. What does a reignited faith in God look like to you? For me, I want to regain my zeal for God—to be tuned-in spiritually to really hear him and to listen when the Holy Spirit is talking to me. (I tend to be heavy on the talking and light on the listening). I want to have a greater hunger to study and follow God's Word, with an anticipatory desire to dig deeper for fresh revelation. And I want to have a fresh compassion for the lost, accompanied by a boldness to share the good news of the gospel with them.

We want to be ignited to walk out our faith in Jesus with boldness and zeal, regardless of the storms raging around us, the stress overtaking us, or the weariness making us want to quit. For that to happen, we need the power of the Holy Spirit. Without a doubt, the Holy Spirit ignites faith. We just need to plug into him.

Too often, the Holy Spirit gets a bad rap among followers of Christ. A lot of people are afraid of him, thinking anything associated with the Holy Spirit is weird. But the Holy Spirit is not a weird, mystical sidenote to God in the Scriptures. The Holy Spirit is the third person of the Trinity—he *is* God. He cannot be separated from God the Father and God the Son. Without the Holy Spirit, we would have no faith at all, and we could do absolutely nothing of any eternal value.

To get where we want to be at the end of our spiritual pilgrimage, we need the Holy Spirit and the Bible, God's Word. Our own strength and wisdom will only carry us so far, leaving us stranded and lost. I've discovered in my own journey that God doesn't usually just zap me with blazing faith because I ask for it. The flame of faith is fanned a little more with each step of obedience, trust, repentance, and worship as I pursue him. It is an orderly process. The Holy Spirit is our guide, and God's Word gives directions for the journey.

God isn't handing us an old-school map as we set out on this spiritual quest or journey, but we do have his Word. It's a good thing his directions are more reliable than the ones the lady in my GPS gives me! We can trust God to show us the way we need to go.

## Which Way Do I Go?

On a recent mission to Myanmar and Vietnam, I was to meet up with my friend in Myanmar. Nancy is a good friend and ministry partner—we often travel together on missions around the world. She was leading a team and had gone on a week ahead, so for my part in this particular mission, I was traveling alone. Which way was I to go?

On such a long journey, I really needed to get all my flights in order. And believe me, there were a bunch of them. I knew where I wanted to end up, but I had to maneuver through a lot of logistics and pass through different nations to get there. My visas had to be in order, and I had to know where and when I'd change airlines and aircrafts, as well as the times of arrival and departure along the way. You should have seen the flight-tracking app on my phone—it looked like a little kid scribbled lines back and forth across the map of the globe.

Starting out from Arkansas, I flew to Houston, then to Taipei, and finally to Yangon to meet my friend. After a few days in Myanmar, we would travel together with another friend to Vietnam, landing in Ho Chi Minh City, change planes, and go on to Da Nang. Getting all the flights together was just a part of the process. I also had to plan and sort through my return, which took a completely different route. Coordinating all these flights, nations, and time zones was no easy task. My desk was covered with copies of e-tickets, itineraries with highlighted arrival and departure times, and my passport and visas, not to mention all the hotel reservations. Finally, with all my documents in order, I typed out a list to carry with me—an instruction sheet, if you will. When in doubt, I could easily refer to this list, rather than dig through a stack of printed documents while waiting at a counter trying to communicate with someone who spoke a different language.

Thankfully, on this spiritual pilgrimage, we won't have to book any flights on Asian airlines or juggle departure and arrival times (the small airlines seem to change the departure times on a whim). And even better than an "instruction sheet," we'll have God's Word to guide us; it is our GPS (minus the annoying lady that spouts off that she's recalculating if you happen to get a little sidetracked).

That trip had a crazy schedule, but the fruit produced from the trouble and confusion made it all worthwhile. We were blessed to build an incredible spiritual bridge between the two nations, and see lives in the persecuted church touched by God's amazing love. That's the way this pilgrimage will be for us, too. We know where we want to end up, and though the trials of the journey might stretch us, the spiritual benefits will make it all worthwhile.

A flaming heart for God will far outweigh any challenges we might encounter along the way. But in order for us to fan our flames and reignite our faith in God, we need to be committed to the pilgrimage. We'll never reach our destination if we give up and quit the first time we hit a stumbling block or when the truth gets a bit too personal. It would be like being stranded in Mandalay because we didn't want to deal with the airline's impromptu flight change. We need to keep our eyes on the goal and on where we want to end up.

We know the desired destination, but like that mission trip to Asia, we also have to know that there will be a lot of stops and challenges along the way. The Holy Spirit will guide, strengthen, encourage, and equip us with everything we need—he is for us. He desires that we walk in the power of his might even more than we have been. And to do that, we must be willing to grow up a little when it comes to our spiritual eating habits.

## Growing Up

The eating habits of the body of Christ are very much like twenty-first-century American children. Oh boy, I'm probably going to step on some toes here, but I am warning you that I'll be doing some meddling. First, let me say this: I love children, and I love the body of Christ. But there is something wrong with both of their eating habits.

Many children refuse to eat foods that their growing bodies need, like spinach and broccoli, and the body of Christ often does the same thing. Churches are filled with scores of seekers—hungry people who seek the truth but are only fed dessert. They hear a message of God's love, mercy, and grace, and are told they can ask for whatever they want and God will give it to them. The message is a distortion and an incomplete portrayal of God.

The part they are missing is the spinach and broccoli, the hard part of the gospel: repentance and turning away from sin. God is holy and righteous. In the presence of God, sin has no place. I don't know if we are afraid of losing people, upsetting them, or looking judgmental, but sin is barely addressed in many churches; and if it is, there is no conviction to turn from it and repent.

Once people are saved, we continue to nurse them along with milk long after they should have matured and begun to eat solid food. When Paul saw this carnality in the Corinthian church, he addressed their lack of growth with these words: "I gave you milk, not solid food, for you were not yet ready for it. Indeed, you are still not ready" (1 Cor. 3:2 NIV). We need solid food to grow. Paul knew this and wanted to feed it to the Corinthian church, but they were so conditioned to drinking milk that they couldn't handle it.

## Feed on Solid Food

Solid food is the *whole* gospel, including both the sweet and the tough, hard-to-swallow parts. It includes repentance, sacrifice, self-denial, placing others over ourselves, and instruction on how to live the Christian life and draw near to God.

We are the temple of the Holy Spirit (1 Cor. 6:19), and for many of us, our temples need some maintenance. We started well, but life has gotten us a little sidetracked. God is calling us to get our focus back to where it should be: preparing for his imminent return.

If you are offended by the message the preacher is preaching, open your Bible and see if what is being preached is the truth. If it is, apply it. If it isn't, don't be afraid to test it. Read the Scriptures with the understanding that they are the very Word of God. Jesus is the Word. As followers of Jesus Christ, we have committed to obey him. If repentance is needed, repent. If you are on a milk diet in your church, find a church that's dishing up some food you can sink your teeth into.

## I've Got This, God

On the opposite end of the spectrum are those of us who've been around for a while, feeding on steak nearly every day. We've studied the Word of God extensively, and we take our walk with God seriously. The more we experience in our Christian walk, the more confidence we gain . . . in ourselves. It's a road well-traveled, so why bother God? We've got this. Because we've just about seen it all, we become less and less intimidated by life and its challenges and less and less dependent on God. That, too, is a dangerous faith-threatening state to be in.

After studying the Scriptures and learning to apply them to our lives, we sometimes feel like we've gained enough discernment and wisdom in handling the circumstances of life, and without meaning to, we often shove the Holy Spirit out of the way. By our actions and attitudes, we say, "I've got this God. I'll call on you if I need you." We try to handle each situation, completely unaware that judgments, resentments, or callousness has taken root in our hearts.

Without even realizing it, we find ourselves looking at people, sizing them up and plunking them right down into categories: *beyond help, taker, unteachable, needy, full of himself, trouble.* We have no compassion, no prayer, and no time for them. Just because we've been weathered in our life as a Christian doesn't mean we'll handle people and circumstances in a God-honoring fashion. There's a critical difference between street-level wisdom gained from experience and spiritual wisdom gained from the Holy Spirit. God is relational, and that means he cares about people. Remember the two most important commandments? Love God, and love people.

Fanning the flame and reigniting our faith in God is a process that will take commitment and a heart set on the goal. As I said before, the benefits far outweigh any trouble we might encounter on our journeys. In the end, when we have run the course of this pilgrimage, I think we all hope to have hearts ablaze, with a fresh, sincere compassion for people—especially the lost. And to say to God, with all sincerity, "Break my heart for what breaks yours."

## Commitment

My many mission journeys have been riddled with obstacles, hardships, and all sorts of setbacks—fear, discouragement, physical discomfort, difficult people, and sickness (even pink eye). Many times, I wanted to quit, wondering what in the world I was doing there and asking myself, "Who do you think you are?" But in every case, the benefits far outweighed the hardships or obstacles, so long as I finished the course and was obedient along the way.

Once the ticket is purchased for any trip, I'm committed. Take a moment right now to purchase your ticket. The cost will be a little time, some "come to Jesus" honesty with yourself, along with obedience and trust in God. Ultimately, it is God who is setting the course. If you are willing, set this book down right now and make a commitment to this pilgrimage. Pray to your loving Father, and ask him to help you as you set your face like flint—like an unmovable rock—to seek him and take back what the enemy has stolen from you spiritually.

Ask Jesus to give you eyes to see and ears to hear what the Spirit is saying, quickening his Word in your heart. And to help you to be honest with yourself and obedient to Jesus, do whatever he might ask you to do, even if that means letting go and unpacking a few things that pull your heart from him. As you journey, may your smoldering embers be fanned back into a blazing fire. The Word of God and the gift of the Holy Spirit are in you. The result of bringing the two together is a reignited powerful faith in him.

# Chapter 3

# Packing and Unpacking

"Faith, as Paul saw it, was a living,
flaming thing leading to surrender . . ."

—A. W. Tozer

**Now that our tickets are** purchased and our destination is clear, the next step is to pack. Just as you would for any road trip or vacation, you have to pack your bag with whatever you will need for the journey. That's the part I always dread and put off to the last minute. Packing for any trip requires a lot of mental work. It's much more than just the physical labor of throwing stuff in a bag. I have to think through all I will be doing so I can pack appropriately and have everything that is needed. In foreign countries, you can't just run down to the store and pick up what you might have forgotten. If you forget it, you either do without or get creative and improvise.

For example, on a trip to Myanmar, my friend Nancy's eye had become red and irritated. She had eye drops with her, but because light bothered her and because she was worried about infection and getting something in it, she needed an eye patch. Of course, we don't usually carry eye patches with us, but I did have a

Dr. Scholl's footpad designed for calluses on the ball of the foot. It was oval-shaped (the perfect size for an eye), and had sticky tape around the edges to hold it in place. That day, Nancy ministered with a Dr. Scholl's footpad over her eye. Not the best look for newsletter pictures, but the impromptu eye patch did the trick.

I travel quite a bit, but for some reason, my tendency is still to overpack. Without fail, just when I think I'm all finished and ready to zip up my bag, I think of one more thing to throw in, just in case I might need it.

"Need," though, is a relevant term. I do need my passport if I'm traveling to another nation, because they won't let me in without it. Prescription medications are also needed. But there are some things, like my toothbrush, electronic chargers, and clothes, as well as some favorite things that always go with me, that I also consider needs, but that I have at times had to manage without when a bag was lost. Those items make me comfortable, but when I didn't have them, I found I could improvise and manage just fine. I discovered this about myself when I flew to California to visit my dad.

## Shedding Some Weight

In this day of TSA regulations and increased travel expenses, airlines have become pretty unforgiving and persnickety when it comes to their luggage requirements and weight limits. On that short trip to California, I was a tad overweight—in my luggage, of course. "Sorry ma'am, your bag is over the weight limit," said the skycap. As I was checking in with a long line of impatient travelers behind me, this was the last thing I wanted to hear. Few things are more embarrassing than exposing my not-so-neatly packed underwear, pajamas, and clothes on the sidewalk of a busy airport while trying to make a snap decision on what I *don't* need.

Pulling out my cell phone, I quickly called my husband, who had just dropped me off and was now leaving the airport. "Honey, could you circle back around? My bag is too heavy and I need to give you some stuff to take back home."

As I unzipped my suitcase, a lady in red shoes behind me, clearly annoyed at the holdup, tapped her foot while checking the time on her cell phone. Curbside check-in is designed to get savvy travelers quickly on their way by *avoiding* people who hold up the line with their overweight bags.

I was eight pounds over, and the guy at the counter wasn't in a mood for grace. Something had to go. Trying to help, he said, "Jeans! Jeans are heavy . . ." I pulled out my favorite pair of jeans, and he threw them on the scale. "Two and a half pounds!" Really? But do I want to let them go? I was heading to sunny California and probably wouldn't need them there anyway, but you know, a girl likes to have her options. I'd obviously allowed myself too many options, and the jeans started the "to go" pile.

A businessman shifted his weight and I felt the pressure. I had to have my hairdryer and toiletry bag, but did I really need my tea kit? My husband calls me a tea snob, because I love my tea and always have it with me. When traveling, I pack a special bag with my favorite teacup and a variety of black and green teas, sweeteners, spoon, and a few cookies. Feeling the businessman's eyes boring holes into the back of my head, I handed my beloved tea kit to the check-in guy. He tossed it aside with my jeans and mumbled, "another pound."

Scanning the contents of my bag, I knew I'd need the remaining clothes. My outfits were carefully planned for each day I'd be in California to celebrate my dad's eightieth birthday. The only heavy thing left was my big, black, soft, genuine leather study Bible, a birthday gift from my husband. I had a smaller travel Bible in my carry-on and several Bible apps on my phone and iPad, but could I manage a whole week without actually *feeling* the pages of my *real* Bible? Lifting it out of my bag, it tipped the scales at a whopping five pounds!

Harvey rounded the corner and before I had time to give it anymore thought, I zipped up the bag and the guy at the ticket counter helped me load it onto the scale. Grabbing my ticket and fumbling with the rest of my stuff, I was finally on my way with a half-pound to spare. Ironically, as I was handing Harvey my Bible, favorite jeans, and tea kit, I realized these were the three most comforting items in my bag, and I was leaving home without them.

We all surround ourselves with those wonderfully familiar items—the little things in life that make us comfortable and happy. The three items I handed over to my husband bring comfort to me when I'm traveling outside my comfort zone.

Faith is like that. Whenever God stretches us to step beyond our comfort zones, the very things we cling to become the hindrances that weigh us down. Clutter—it's all the extra stuff we cram into our lives to make life easy and comfortable so we seemingly have no need for faith. An uncluttered faith is often an *uncomfortable* faith—because when we let go of the extra stuff, we are left with a greater need to trust in Jesus.

We can get quite cozy with our schedules, routines, affirming friends, entertainment, and the creature comforts of home—even church. And there is nothing wrong with those things, but when our lives are filled with clutter, our intimacy with God suffers. This kind of clutter can be far weightier than a temptation to sin, and that is precisely why God sometimes requires that we let it go.

Like Paul told the Corinthian church: "You say, 'I am allowed to do anything'—but not everything is beneficial" (1 Cor. 10:23 NLT).

Just as throwing a wet blanket on a campfire keeps the flames from breathing, all that extra weight can smother the quiet voice of the Holy Spirit. In the noisy clutter and routine of life, a flame is easily lost or extinguished, causing us to become dull of hearing. When forced to expend a bit more energy in shedding the excess weight, just as I had to do at the airport, we're more apt to listen a little closer to the Holy Spirit because we become more dependent on him. Open ears result in open hearts.

Identifying and removing the excess weight and clutter in our lives is the first step on our pilgrimage toward reigniting our faith in God. We surrender everything in our bags, allowing him to show us what is needed and what is not. This is like taking everything out of the suitcase and spreading it out on floor, examining one item at a time while asking ourselves a few questions. First question: Is this weighing me down? Second: Why am I clinging to it? Finally: What is this excess weight costing me spiritually?

## I Surrender All

Now, to avoid scenarios like the one described above and to keep from paying the extra fee for overweight bags, I keep a luggage scale with me. As a missionary, I've grown accustomed to asking myself, "Is this something I can live without?" I then often jettison the item that would be nice to have but that I can manage without.

I once had a pastor who had a saying for whenever conversation got a bit too personal: "Now you've gone to meddlin'." Well, I'll just give you fair warning—I'm "goin' to meddlin'."

In the chorus of the hymn *I Surrender All,* we sing with all sincerity:

I surrender all
I surrender all
All to Thee my blessed Savior
I surrender all[1]

From the depths of our hearts and with all sincerity we worship God singing those words. But at the same time, our human nature, or flesh, is humming a totally different tune. It goes something like this:

I can't surrender all, but
I surrender most
Most to Thee, my blessed Savior,
I surrender most

A. W. Tozer once said, "Faith, as Paul saw it, was a living, flaming thing leading to surrender . . ."[2] And that's true. But when our faith isn't flaming, it is kind of hard to see what we need to surrender. The things we cling to, familiar things that make us happy and comfortable, aren't bad in and of themselves, but they do tend to weigh pretty heavily on the spiritual scales. Because we are so used to having them around, it may take some prying to get our white-knuckle grip to loosen up and let them go. Faith truly is the living, flaming thing that leads us to surrender all to Jesus, because when we have faith, we also have trust. Let's ask God to help us uncover some of the hidden things that weigh us down and smother our faith.

## Uncovering Pride

Pride is one of the weightier items in anyone's bag, and God warns us about pride in many places in his Word. Look at Romans 12:3

from the New Living Translation: "I give each of you this warning: Don't think you are better than you really are. Be honest in your evaluation of yourselves, measuring yourselves by the faith God has given us."

My bag was bulging with judgments and pride I didn't even realize I was carrying. The Holy Spirit had to point out some serious excess weight I had stuffed into my heart and show me how this carried over into my ministry. I'll go ahead and make myself a little transparent here to give you just a small sample of how subtle pride can be in our lives.

I was asked to do a blended family workshop in a local church based on my book *Tying the Family Knot: Meeting the Challenges of a Blended Family*. The group was small, probably no more than fifteen people. After going through the material and talking about the challenges of blending a family, we had a casual time for questions and answers and for visiting one-on-one.

Several of the attendees asked for advice on how to work through some of the emotional conflicts of blending with a difficult exspouse or of visitation rights. The discussion was going well, with almost everyone comparing stories and experiences, discussing solutions and ideas for solutions—some that worked and others that didn't.

But there was one young woman who stuck to me like glue. She tearfully talked about her family, her husband, and her stepchildren, hoping I could give her answers to fix everything that was wrong. She had issues far beyond normal blended family conflicts. I didn't know her personally, but I knew her by her manner, and without even taking time to listen to her heart or pray, I placed her into the "needy" category. With a smile plastered onto my face,

I offered a few suggestions, and invited her to come to my office where we could talk in greater detail—essentially dismissing her.

I'd like to say I took a minute to pull her aside and pray with her and really listen to her heart, but I didn't. After the class, my husband, who came with me to the workshop to help set up, told me (or perhaps I should say, scolded me) about brushing off that young woman who was asking for my help. He had been observing from the sidelines and noticed my lack of compassion. If my husband was disturbed by my attitude, I can just imagine how grieved the Holy Spirit must have been.

The mirror of God's Word reveals that we have a deceitful and desperately sick heart that needs daily rescue (Jer. 17:9). We deceive ourselves when we move into greater dependence on our own wisdom, knowledge, influence, name, reputation, and even knowledge of the Scriptures. The tighter we cling to them, the less dependent we become on God, deceiving ourselves into believing we have it all together. Without actually saying it, our actions and attitudes declare to God, "I've got this!"

Many have said "knowledge is power," and it's true—the more you know, the more you can accomplish. But knowledge must never be confused with faith. Our faith comes from God, not from ourselves and what we know, our abilities, or experiences. When we rely solely on what we know or have experienced, there isn't enough room left in our bags for faith.

This subtle deception can be a lot heavier in a believer's life than we might realize, weighing so much more than it might appear. I know this for myself—I had to take a hard, honest look at my own heart to even know it was there, because it was hidden somewhere between the layers of the faith and godly wisdom I'd gained in my years as a follower of Jesus Christ. Once uncovered,

I had to lighten myself of that burden. Pride is sin, and the only way for me to unpack it was to repent.

But once that pride was jettisoned from my bag, I discovered two spiritual changes in myself. The first was that I had a greater capacity to love people, and the second was that I found myself praying more whenever I talked to people who appeared to be needier than others—this drew me closer to God and increased the intensity of my spiritual flame.

## Pride Disguised

Pride can also disguise itself by taking on many forms in a believer's life. Pastors ask other pastors, "How many are you running these days?" Meaning, how many people are you gathering in to hear you preach? But just in case you think this is only a problem for ministers, think about the times you've dropped names or shared "revelations you've gleaned from Scriptures" with the purpose of looking spiritual to someone else.

I'm not saying all Christians are full of themselves and prideful—I'm just snooping around in your bag, meddling a little bit, and asking you to honestly look at those subtle sins hidden between the layers of godly wisdom. If the Holy Spirit reveals something that might be weighing you down, I'm asking you to pull it out, shake it out, and take a good, hard, honest look at it. Then, if needed, repent and get rid of it. The blood of Jesus cleanses us, but when we permit these hidden sins to remain, like a bad apple, they have a way of spoiling the rest of the good things in our lives.

## I Can Do It Myself

When my son was a toddler, he wouldn't let me help him with anything. He always scoffed at me and said, "I can do it myself!" He was determined to do everything himself. But some things were just too much for him. I had to let him try and fail, and to finally become so frustrated that he'd ask me to help. I guess we're not much different than a toddler when it comes to being independent.

Like I said earlier, I have a tendency to overpack, and I guess this same tendency carries over into life, because I'm a "fix it" kind of person and a perfectionist. This is a bad combination when the Holy Spirit isn't in control. People like me get the job done, and we do it well. But we tend to overdo, overcommit, and overrun others who are there to help by micromanaging them.

Somehow, people like me think we can do it all ourselves. When we hold the reins so tightly, no one else can come alongside to help, even though God has sent them to us. And why do we hold the reins so tightly? Because we don't trust others to do the job the way we think it should be done. This hinders others from stepping up and into the work God may be calling them to do; and of course, we can't do the job as well because we spread ourselves too thin. The end result is discouragement and frustration all around.

## Let's Do Lunch

When I first started out in ministry, I led a ladies Bible study at my church every Thursday. For years, this study was held at 10:00 A.M. The woman who had always led the study could no longer do it, so seeing the need and feeling a call to teach, I approached my pastor and began my ministry to women. I absolutely loved women's ministry, and still do.

The Bible studies went very well, but I noticed that when we were finished, some of the women went out to lunch together, but others couldn't afford it. It was easy to see that they felt a little left out. Women like to chat and have time together to talk about life. It's in our DNA.

After praying about it, I went to the pastor to see if we could change the time for Bible study, making it an hour longer, and if we could provide an inexpensive salad lunch so everyone would be included in a fellowship time afterwards. With his permission and a budget, I made the announcement. I then proceeded to get up early on Thursdays, shop for food, prepare lunch, teach the class, serve lunch, and then clean up afterward. It was a lot of work, but everyone loved the new format.

Because the perfectionist in me wanted it to be a special time for the ladies, I served lunch with the church's nice plates, glassware, and silverware (I really had no idea how crazy this was!). Of course, this meant that everything had to be washed and put away afterward. To add a personal touch, I even made little centerpieces for the tables.

After a few weeks, one of the women, now one of my dearest friends, approached me. "Terri, why don't you let the ladies help with lunch and the cleanup instead of doing it all yourself? And why don't you use disposable plates and cups instead of having to wash everything?" I brushed her off, thinking I could handle the work and that it wouldn't be as nice using paper plates. Cynthia persisted, and every Thursday, she came early to help and stayed after to clean up. She also recruited others to help. I eventually relented about the disposables, but held tightly to the reins of control.

Everyone loved the changes and our group grew in numbers, but as the season changed from summer to fall, salads weren't quite as appealing for lunch, and there was talk of doing soup or chili. Of course with soup, you need bread, and because we are in the South, any "real" meal is followed by dessert—all of this put even more on my plate. During the fellowship time, the ones who liked to cook talked about their meal ideas, and the ones who liked to decorate talked about creative table décor. They even talked about doing weekly themes. *I* was the only thing holding them back from living out their God-given gifts of hospitality.

I was wearing myself out by trying to do everything, and because the lunch and fellowship time had become so important, the time I'd spend with Jesus in prayer and preparation for the Bible study was often cut short. Our ladies Bible study and fellowship time was good, but my spiritual health was suffering.

## Letting Go of My Ego

It was time for me to let go and unpack my ego. When I did, the ladies ran with it, creating a sign-up sheet to prepare weekly lunches and another for cleanup. Every week was a surprise, and all the work was done without me dotting a single "i" or crossing a single "t."

Ladies Bible study and fellowship time was a huge hit, and the relationships that developed out of it are still intact all these years later. Favorite Thursday recipes were compiled into a cookbook, *The Thursday Cuisine*, and I still use those recipes today. By unpacking my perfectionism and ego, not only did I get out of the way for others to step into their gifts, but I could also focus my attention back on Jesus and my teaching—the work God had called me to.

What I learned from that experience is that it's God who puts people in our lives. "He makes the whole body fit together perfectly" (Eph. 4:16 NLT), as the Scripture says. Everyone has gifts that God wants to develop and use. We stifle those gifts in others when we micromanage. Jesus is all about building up and growing his body for doing kingdom work. It's not our work—it's God's. Ephesians 4:11–12 says, "Now these are the gifts Christ gave to the church: the apostles, the prophets, the evangelists, and the pastors and teachers. Their responsibility is to equip God's people to do his work and build up the church, the body of Christ" (NLT).

My example is a ladies Bible study, but the same has applied to everything I do. I still have a desire for excellence in my work, but God has taught me to delegate and allow the people he sends to walk alongside me the freedom to do their work without me watching over them. As they operate in their gifts, they will be built up and equipped to do the work they are called to do, celebrating their successes while learning and growing from their mistakes.

If we don't unpack this kind of excess weight, the cost is our own weariness and, eventually, burnout. Yes, we can do all things through Christ who strengthens us, but we are his body, made up of many members—each having its own function, but working together (1 Cor. 12:12). One hand can't do all the lifting alone. It needs the other hand, the arms, the legs, and the back. As in the body of Christ, we need each other.

What we hope to gain on this pilgrimage is a vibrant and ongoing relationship with our God—one that calls us to look to him before those challenging, bad, or hard circumstances occur in our lives. By appropriately packing our bags, we will walk out our faith with our spiritual ears bent toward him, no matter what season of life we might be in.

## Notes

[1]Judson W. Van DeVenter, "I Surrender All," Hymnary.org, 1896, public domain, http://www.hymnary.org/text/all_to_jesus_i_surrender.

[2]A.W. Tozer, *Paths to Power: Living in the Spirit's Fullness* (Nyack, New York: Christian and Missionary Alliance, 1940), chapter 6, Kindle edition.

# Chapter 4

# In and Out of Season

"For everything there is a season,
   a time for every activity under heaven."

—Ecclesiastes 3:1 NLT

**Every trip is different,** and, therefore, packing requirements change. When I travel to speak, my packing looks a lot different than when I pack for a mission trip. And when I pack for working an event with my husband's business, my bag looks nothing like it does when I'm packing for a conference. Life in Christ is like that too. As I write about below, our friend Dale's gift of music wasn't taken away; it was just unpacked during his pastoral season. Then it was repacked for the season that followed.

Along the way in our journeys, we gain a lot of great things: biblical knowledge, wisdom, influence, reputation, skills, and good names for ourselves. The road we travel in life is also filled with experiences, different kinds of people, and difficult circumstances we've had to overcome. We all have our victories, as well as lessons learned from our mistakes and failures. God uses everything we've experienced in our lives—nothing is wasted. Certain gifts and experiences may not be needed or used in every season, but they're always there.

I love how Romans 11:29 reads in the New Living Translation: "For God's gifts and his call can never be withdrawn." Some gifts are needed for a season, and others are not, but when God calls us or gives us a gift, it is for life.

God often brings us through seasons in our lives, and different seasons require different gifts. This doesn't mean we must use every gift in every season. In fact, God often tests us to see how tightly we cling to our gifts. (Remember Abraham and his only son, Isaac?) The gifts God gives us can seemingly become more important than God, and thus a hindrance to faith. When we allow this to happen, the life can be sucked right out of our spiritual flame.

My good friend told me how God loosened his tight-knuckled grip on something he loved doing for the Lord. Dale recently retired as executive pastor of his church in North Carolina, but before God called him into pastoring, he had a singing ministry that involved going to other churches and performing concerts. "I love to sing, and get so full just sharing music and songs with folks," Dale told me. In fact, it was because of his love for music that we met. He was picking guitar and we were singing hymns with a small group of friends at an event we were all attending.

Dale told me a story of how music was gone from his ministry when he accepted the call to pastor. It was just gone. He said he didn't get another call to sing in any church. In fact, he wasn't even asked to sing in his own church. In his words, "God unpacked and repacked me again." Interestingly, several years later, after God told him his time there as pastor was completed and it was time to retire, the music returned. Once he stepped down as pastor, he was asked to sing quite regularly again, opening revivals, singing songs with tracks, and playing his guitar. The music was back.

Many of us hang on to our God-given and ordained gifts and talents as if they are the only way God can use us. When we refuse to loosen our grip, clinging to every gift in every season, we get into trouble. We might think we are bringing a "sacrifice" to God with a gift, but if God is asking us to surrender it to him, it becomes disobedience. Sometimes God tests us to see what place our gift has in our life, like he tested Abraham when he asked him to sacrifice Isaac.

Abraham loved Isaac, as he was the promised child he had waited years for—his heir. But when God told Abraham to climb the mountain and sacrifice Isaac, he didn't argue or procrastinate. Scripture says he got up early the next morning, chopped the wood for the burnt offering, grabbed a couple servants, and headed out on his journey with Isaac. He got up early! He was quick to obey, and even willing to give up the most important thing in the world to him.

When they got to the top of the mountain and Abraham lifted the knife over his precious gift, his only son, God provided a substitutional sacrifice, and Isaac lived. God said to Abraham, "I swear by myself . . . that because you have done this and have not withheld your son, your only son, I will surely bless you . . ." (Gen. 22:16–17 NIV). This same principle and blessing applies to us. When we don't withhold our gifts and the things we love so much, no matter what they might be, God will bless us.

## Do I Need This Now?

God has given each one of us exactly what we need to fulfill his purposes in each season of life. But seasons, and our needs during them, differ. For instance, if I were packing for a trip to the Bahamas, I wouldn't need a winter coat, but I will probably need it when the temperature drops. For now, in the Bahamas, it would just take up a lot of room and make my bag too heavy to carry.

God allowed us our particular upbringings and histories, both good and bad, to shape us. He placed us in our geographical spots on the earth and imparted to us gifts, talents, and experiences. He even allowed the challenges and trials we've walked through to strengthen, teach, and guide us. By the time he calls us to do something for him, we are fully equipped. Whether that call is in formal ministry, mission work, intercession, raising up godly children, going to school, driving a church bus, teaching, or any other vocation, we have what we need.

When we try to force the use of a God-given gift into a place it isn't needed, our work for the kingdom of God is not as effective. And remember, Jesus taught us to pray, "Thy kingdom come, Thy will be done, On earth as it is in heaven" (Matt. 6:10 RSV). It's about building his kingdom and his will, not ours. Stubbornly refusing to surrender all to Jesus opens the door for the enemy (Satan) to enter in and sour our attitudes with God and other people. This, of course, affects our relationships and spiritual flames.

At this point in your pilgrimage and season, ask God to help you with your packing *and* unpacking. We all need the Holy Spirit to help us, because along with all the good and needed items, our bags can be overpacked and stuffed with good things that aren't needed—unnecessary weight that can be a hindrance to this particular season of life.

# Chapter 5

# Who Am I?

"If you are humble, nothing will touch you, neither praise
nor disgrace, because you know what you are."

—Mother Teresa

"Who am I? Who am I?" Pastor John Mubiru repeated the question
over and over again as he flipped the light switches, ran his hands
across the smooth, thick comforter on the bed, and turned on
a the large flat-screen television. Coming from a background of
poverty in Uganda, he never imagined staying in such luxury as
this five-star hotel in Nairobi.

At the end of our mission trip in Uganda, God blessed us with
the funds to take pastor John and his wife, Monique, on a safari
with the rest of our U.S. team on our way back home. We had spent
a grueling two weeks working from sunup until sundown, and
we were excited about our stopover in Kenya to see the beautiful
animals. When booking the safari, we had no idea the hotel would
be so nice—it was included in our travel package. They just told us
we would be picked up at the airport and escorted to a partnering

hotel for the night, and then leave for the safari the next morning. I kind of expected it to be like the guesthouse we stayed at in Uganda, not a five-star hotel.

In repeating this question, "Who am I?" Pastor John did what many of us do: compare ourselves to something or someone else. He obviously did not see himself as one who deserved that kind of luxury. Even though he and his wife, Monique, live comfortably by Ugandan standards, he still saw himself through the eyes of a boy raised in the bush. His question could just as well have been "What am I doing here?" or "Who do I think I am, staying in this high-class hotel? I'm just a poor boy from the bush country."

## Here Am I

But pastor John's "Who am I?" question was asked out of humility and praise to God for an unexpected blessing. I had a similar experience after God called me to be a missionary to Africa. When I got home from my first trip to Uganda, I knew (but pretended not to know) God was calling me to be a missionary. I felt completely inadequate and unqualified, and looked for someone to agree that God would never use me. During the course of a conversation with friends who were involved in a missions ministry, I kept asking the same question: "Who am I?" All I could see was my lack of education and my inexperience—all the practical reasons I didn't feel qualified.

After asking "Who am I?" for the umpteenth time, my friend finally jumped up and nearly shouted, "Don't ask, 'Who am I?' Just say, 'Here am I!' If God wants to use a donkey, or someone like me, who am I to question him? It's not about you or me; it is about the people and work God is calling us to. God qualifies the called. It is about trusting him and being obedient."

What does all of this have to do with reigniting our faith in God? More than you might realize. How we see ourselves colors how we see others and, ultimately, how we see God. And that, of course, affects our faith in God.

## People-Pleasing

Think about the reason God rejected King Saul from being king over the people of Israel. He was a people-pleaser instead of a God-pleaser—fearing man more than he feared God. Always concerned about how people saw him and what they thought of him, King Saul was intimidated and threatened by people. This controlled him and became his downfall.

When Saul was chosen to be king, the Spirit of God was upon him to rule the people of Israel. He had many victories and the people followed him wholeheartedly. Life was good.

But two years into his reign, Saul had a major run-in with his archenemies, the Philistines. His son, Jonathan, attacked a garrison of the Philistines, and because Saul was so proud, he announced the victory to everyone. The Israelites cheered, but when the Philistines heard about it, they rose with a vengeance. They showed up with "thirty thousand chariots, and six thousand horsemen, and people as the sand which is on the sea shore in multitude" (1 Sam. 13:5 KJV). In fear, the people of Israel ran for the hills and caves to hide.

Samuel, the prophet who anointed Saul as king, told him to wait seven days to offer sacrifices to the Lord before they went into battle. Saul waited, but when seven days came and went, the pressure of the people scattering proved to be too much for him. Saul compromised his faith in God by taking matters into his own hands. Instead of waiting for Samuel, he went ahead and offered the sacrifice on his own, which was completely against the law of God.

Repeatedly throughout his reign, Saul let his fear of man control his actions. The last straw was when God told him to completely destroy the Amalekites, sparing nothing. He destroyed everything that was worthless, but let the people bring back the best of the spoil and take the king prisoner. When Samuel asked why Saul didn't obey God's command, he said "the people" spared the best to sacrifice to God (1 Sam. 15:15 ESV). Saul was the king. He called the shots. But his fear of man stole his faith in God.

## Stolen Faith

If you'll give me just a little liberty here, I would like to pause and ask you what I've had to ask myself. Have you ever allowed what people think of or say about you steal your faith? Here is a scenario: You know someone who has never given their life to Jesus, and they are lying near death in the hospital. You have a very strong conviction to go share the gospel and pray for them. You *know*, without a doubt, that God wants you to do this. So you arrange your day and go to the hospital to pray for them. But when you get there, the room is filled with family, most of whom are unbelievers. What do you do?

When I first became a Christian and my spiritual flame was blazing hot, I would not have hesitated for even a second to share the gospel, no matter who was there. I would have been respectful of the family and asked if I could pray, glad that other unsaved family members might also find salvation in Jesus as they listened. But when our faith is a flickering flame, it is easy to back away from this call to duty because of the fear of what someone might think of us, even at the cost of a lost soul. No wonder Jesus says if we are lukewarm, he will spew us out of his mouth (Rev. 3:16).

It is easy to talk about God among fellow Christians, or from a pulpit where it is expected, but what about in times of confrontation or pressure from an unbelieving world? Compromise is an easy out. When God doesn't answer right away, do you compromise and back away from what you know you should do, to do whatever it takes to make people happy? When we do this, we are no longer living by faith. Our flesh loves to be stroked, but it hates disapproval. Like quicksand, this trap will suck us deeper and deeper until our faith in God is an illusion. We tell ourselves we have faith in God, but in reality, we have little to none.

Samuel's response to Saul's excuse is the same for us: "What is more pleasing to the LORD: your burnt offerings and sacrifices or your obedience to his voice? Listen! Obedience is better than sacrifice, and submission is better than offering the fat of rams" (1 Sam. 15:22 NLT).

## The Walking Dead

"Who am I?" is a universal question, and how we answer it depends greatly on our faith in God. If we trust God with our lives, we become small in our own sight, and that's okay. A spirit of humility is based in the knowledge that God has our best interests at heart, because we are confident in his unconditional love for us. It doesn't matter if no one shows appreciation for our song, our teaching, or our good deed. And it also doesn't matter if they heap praises on us, because we know it is only because of God that we can do what we do. I love this quote from Mother Teresa: "If you are humble, nothing will touch you, neither praise nor disgrace, because you know what you are."[1] Humility is a value we tend to disregard, because we are more focused on being appreciated, noticed, or admired.

When we disregard humility, we also disregard our faith and trust in God. But when we know who and what we are, as Mother Teresa suggested, the words people say or don't say and the things they do or don't do have no effect on us because we are only looking for God's approval. We are dead in Christ—we no longer live, Christ lives in us. Galatians 2:20 (NIV) puts it this way: "I have been crucified with Christ and I no longer live, but Christ lives in me. The life I now live in the body, I live by faith in the Son of God, who loved me and gave himself for me."

I once heard a preacher say that if we are crucified with Christ, we are dead, and dead men don't bleed. They don't get offended or hurt when they are kicked to the curb. They're dead. And if we have been crucified with Christ, we also have no need of praise and approval. As followers of Christ, we live life in a flesh and blood body, but we are hidden in him. It isn't about what this fleshly body wants, it is about what Jesus wants—his will, not mine, because my life is his life, and we are not our own.

## The Enemy's Scheme

We have an enemy. Drawing us in to looking at our own qualifications and abilities to do God's work and obey his call is one of Satan's subtle tactics to derail the work of God, and ultimately our faith. When we are doing the work, even with good motives and obedience to our call, the scheme of the enemy is to get our focus on the approval of people. Even though our gifts, talents, and callings are from God, and even though he is the one who equips and enables us to do his will, it feels good when we receive recognition. Everyone likes to be appreciated. A pat on the back, a compliment on how great your preaching or singing was, or any public recognition for your kingdom accomplishments—it doesn't take much to make us humans crave more, or disappointed when we do a good job and it isn't appreciated or is overlooked.

Over time, if we become lax in the time we spend with God in prayer and the study of his Word, the focus of our hearts becomes all about making ourselves look good to people (more on this in a later chapter). We can give God the glory with our lips, but if people see us in a different light than we'd hoped, look out.

Think about it. If you do something good, like preach a good sermon, teach a good lesson, sing a beautiful praise song, or landscape the church property, and you receive several positive comments and just one negative word, which sticks out in your mind? Which do you focus your attention on? All the good comments? Or the negative one? The good comments are nice, but that one negative word sticks out like a sore thumb hit with a hammer. The level of our faith and its flame will determine our response. When we choose to please people, the craving for acceptance can control us the same as it did King Saul.

## Somebodies and Nobodies

Another downside to people-pleasing is when we begin to either believe we are the best thing to come along since sliced bread—a real "somebody"; or, just the opposite, when we feel like a failure, like a real "nobody." King Saul would probably answer the question "Who am I?" by saying he was "somebody."

When someone asks "Who are you?" how do we respond? Well, that depends on who is asking and who we perceive them to be. There are two general types of responses. The first type of response comes from someone who wants to be seen as a "somebody," and the second type comes from someone who wants to hide because they see themselves as a "nobody." One wants others to see their value; the other feels they have no value.

## Somebodies

For now, let's take the "somebodies," who seldom just give their name and leave it at that. Of course, they want to relate to whomever it is they are talking with, but more importantly, their human nature wants to be perceived as having value, so they look for opportunities to interject more valuable information about themselves—what they do, who they know, or what they've accomplished.

"I'm Seymore Green . . . what do I do? Oh, I'm an investment banker with New York Big Finance Group." That would be an example for a businessman, but people in ministry do the same thing. "I'm Reverend B. Good from First Church. You may have seen us on TV." We love to put our best foot forward, no matter our vocation—whether we excel in sports, business, ministry, education, cooking, homemaking, building, art, politics, public service . . . whatever. What we do and what we've accomplished becomes our identity and, subsequently, our value.

## Nobodies

"Nobodies" are on the opposite side of the spectrum. Often intimidated by the "somebodies," "nobodies" have trouble finding any value in themselves at all, perhaps because of past failures, abuses, or insecurities. They usually prefer to stay hidden in the shadows, giving their name when asked, but little more.

In Christ, we all have value, value which isn't measured by performance or the standards set by humans. Jesus died for all, and all have sinned and fallen short of his glory. It is only by his acceptance and love for us that we can do anything. That is Christianity 101. We can't *do* any more, *be* any more, *pray* any more, or even *study God's Word* any more to make God love us more than he already does.

God's love is complete, and this has nothing to do with what we do or don't do. His love is the same, whether we've won a million souls for the kingdom or just prayed to receive salvation through faith in Jesus. That's the plain and simple truth. It's hard to grasp how deeply he loves us and how much he values us—by God's grace and by our faith in Jesus, we are *all* "somebodies."

Resist the enemy's scheme, and take your eyes off yourself and off the people you've been trying to impress, and put them back on Jesus. In God's eyes, anybody and everybody is equal. "Somebodies" and "nobodies" do not exist. Like God told Samuel when he was anointing David to be king, "man looks on the outward appearance, but the LORD looks on the heart" (1 Sam. 16:7 ESV). God is looking for people whose hearts are after his heart—those who love and obey him. We are all "somebodies" in his eyes.

## God Sees Cookies

Have you ever thought about how God sees us? Most of us tend to look through the lens of whatever we are going through at the moment. If we are having financial trouble, we only see lack. If we get an unexpected raise at work, we see blessing. If our marriage is bad, we see hurt, anger, and disappointment. If the guy we were hoping would call calls, we see romance. If we get a bad report from the doctor, we see sickness or even death. But if the report is good, we see healing. Emotional highs and lows go along with the challenges and blessings of life. God doesn't have a lens to color what he sees. He sees everything we are walking through as necessary ingredients for the person he is creating us to be.

Recently, our pastor gave an interesting sermon on sanctification—the process we go through on our way to being transformed into the likeness of Christ. He asked us to think about the process a baker goes through to make cookies. When the baker looks at all the ingredients, he doesn't see flour, sugar, eggs, salt, butter, vanilla, and whatever else the recipe calls for—he sees cookies.

The baker knows he'll have to break a few eggs and do a little sifting. He knows just how much sugar, butter, and vanilla to blend in. It is all part of the process. But in the end, the baker knows he'll be pulling something wonderful from the oven. And the aroma from those fresh-baked cookies will draw others to want to hang out in the kitchen with the baker.

God, like the baker, has the recipe for our lives. He knows what it will take to make us who he designed us to be, but he isn't focused on the ingredients, because he sees cookies. We all go through sifting to remove impurities, and our brokenness can be compared to the baker breaking the eggs to get to the good stuff that's inside the shell. Life stirs in the bitter, salty hard times as well as sugar-sweet blessings. The process isn't much fun at times, but everything is necessary for the recipe. No one likes to take a beating, but once all the ingredients are combined and they go through the fire to be baked, we can finally see ourselves the way God has seen us from the beginning. God saw the finished product of cookies, not just raw ingredients or half-baked cookie dough.

Baking cookies might be a simplistic analogy for some of the serious issues you've had to walk through in life. There's nothing simple about divorce, death, financial burdens, betrayals, cancer, or infertility, but truthfully, if we can hang in there and go the distance with God, he will make something good out of it.

"You're His" is the answer to the not-so-simple question of "Who Am I?" You don't have to qualify or prove yourself to anyone, not even to God. God is for you. If other people see you as a "somebody" or a "nobody," what is that to you? Your life is hidden in Christ.

### Note

[1]Mother Teresa, *No Greater Love* (Novato, CA: New World Library, 1997), 55, Kindle edition.

# Chapter 6

# Where Is Your Faith?

"Faith is the gaze of a soul upon a saving God."

—A. W. Tozer

One of the amazing things about God is that even though we freak out and give up when things go spinning out of our control, he doesn't. Do you remember when the disciples were crossing the lake in a boat and a sudden storm came up? All the disciples could see were waves, wind, and certain death. Remarkably, Jesus was napping in the hull and woke to his buddies screaming, "We're all gonna die!" Shaking off his sleep, Jesus got up, and as if scolding a rebellious child, he spoke directly to the winds and waves to be still—and they obeyed. Immediately, everything calmed down and all was well. Storms don't rattle Jesus, because he is in control of every storm (even the ones in our lives). After calming the storm, he turned his eyes to the disciples and asked, "Have you no faith?" (Mark 4:40 RSV).

That really is the question, isn't it? Where is our faith? What happened to it? Why do our personal storms grip us with such fear? Jesus's question leads me to ask another. Could the disciples have calmed the storm? Could I have? While in the midst of raging waves crashing against us, is it possible to stand up with all the faith needed to speak peace into our storm? I believe it is.

Earlier, I told you about the confidence I had as a new believer. Huge mountains were moved and some powerful hurricanes were calmed from knees bent in front of my old, gray chair. If God said it in his Word, I believed it. You've probably experienced some mountain-moving faith moments in your Christian walk too. Somehow, over time, my faith seems to have weakened, or at least it doesn't seem to be what it used to be.

We can't just conjure up faith as if we could lift ourselves out of a pit by our bootstraps. Faith is a gift imparted to each of us from God—a truly amazing gift (1 Cor. 12:9). The Greek word for faith is *pistis*. It is a divinely implanted confidence and trust in God.

If we had that mountain-moving faith to believe in the past, it is still in us. My Bible says, "God's gifts and his call can never be withdrawn" (Rom. 11:29 TLB). The gift of faith, the divinely implanted confidence and trust I once had in God, is still there. It just needs to be fanned back into a flame.

## Help Me! I'm Sinking!

Just a little faith goes a long way. Jesus himself said if our faith is even as small as a mustard seed, we can move mountains (Matt. 17:20). Peter demonstrated this mustard seed faith in another storm when he climbed out of the boat to join Jesus walking on the water (Matt. 14:29). Okay, maybe he didn't take much of a stroll on the waves, but he did have enough divine confidence in Jesus to get out of the boat and take at least a few steps. That's more faith than the other disciples showed.

Of course, Peter's faith was short-lived when he took his eyes off Jesus and started looking at the waves. When Peter realized he was going down and that the only thing on the whole planet that could help him was standing right in front on him, he cried out for help because he thought he was sinking. I'm not much different than Peter in that respect. Jesus is always right there when I'm going through a storm, but I can't see past the waves. I love that Jesus immediately grabbed Peter and held on tight. He didn't hesitate for even a second, or let him drown. He got him back into the boat where it was safe, and then he calmed the winds. Jesus is for us, so he's not condemning us when we start to sink—he does for us what he did for Peter. I think this is the way it is when we look at our storms and circumstances and start sinking. When we realize and acknowledge that Jesus is the answer, he immediately stretches out his hand and takes hold of us.

But listen to what Jesus said to Peter at the moment he began to sink: "O you of little faith, why did you doubt?" (Matt. 14:31 ESV). Let me give you my own paraphrase for what Jesus was saying to Peter (and to us) for whenever our faith gets sidetracked by life and its storms. "O you who still have so little confidence in me, what made you look back at the storm? You were already walking on the water." Peter had the gift of faith, but his level of faith at that time was low, just as Jesus said.

We've had water-walking moments in our lives too, so why do we doubt that Jesus will take care of us? We want to be like Peter when he got out of the boat, but too often, we find ourselves sinking like Peter when the winds and waves of life start kicking up around us.

I can remember that sinking feeling when I went through a particularly difficult time about three or four years after my "old, gray chair" great faith experiences. We moved across the country and the hard times began. At the time, it seemed like my trials weren't just trials—they seemed to have become my lot in life. There were many tearful prayers when I repeatedly asked the Lord if I would ever know joy. I wanted to quit, but didn't know what to quit to make it better. I was just stuck. I'll spare you all the sordid details, because you probably have your own "lot in life" story and know exactly what that despair feels like.

Putting my toe of faith in the water, I tried climbing out of the boat, with my eyes fixed on Jesus. Trusting him, I took a step outside my little boat, to a safe place to share some of my situation with a friend from church. After pouring my heart out, my friend prayed with me and then patted me on the back and quoted Romans 8:28: "And we know that all things work together for good to those who love God, to those who are the called according to *His* purpose" (NKJV).

While I knew it was true (that God would somehow make something good come of the situation, someday), all I could see and feel at that moment was hurt and brokenness. I felt the waves crashing around me and down I went, sinking into despair. I know my friend meant well, but the last thing I wanted to hear was a "pat" answer from the Scriptures. I wanted God to fix the problems swirling around me, not tell me it would all work out in the end. Jesus grabbed me and kept me from drowning, but at that point, my faith was like Peter's—little.

I could have given up, but God wasn't finished with me. He was answering my prayers, just not in the way and timing I would have chosen. God knew the end from the beginning. Even though I couldn't see or feel anything but despair, the Holy Spirit was doing something in me and for me. Those trials were some of the hardest I've ever faced. It seemed like I was being broken and sifted daily. But later, after the trials were behind me, the faithfulness and trustworthiness of God were confirmed to me by the Holy Spirit, increasing my level of faith. When the next storm hit, I was a little more confident to take a few more steps out onto the water.

## Increase My Faith

I'm adding my voice to the disciples in asking Jesus to increase my faith. We are all in different places in our walk with Jesus, and we are not all where we think we could or should be in our level of faith. Maybe that's you, and maybe that's precisely the reason you picked up this book in the first place. The good news is that wherever we might be in our level of faith, Jesus is there with us and for us, cheering us on to become the person he created us to be so we can fulfill the plans he has for us.

At this stage in my walk with God, I don't want Jesus to have to rescue me from drowning. I don't want him to say, "O you of little faith." When he looks at me, I want him to see "great faith"—faith with enough confidence in him that I can just hop out of the boat, take his hand, and go for a stroll on the water, despite the storms raging all around. I'm not there yet, but I'm not sinking so quickly as I once was, either.

## Promise Keeper

Little faith grows into great faith, day-by-day and year-by-year, as God shows himself to be faithful to his promises. He keeps his word—whatever he says, he will do. God is a promise keeper. Though it's difficult to count all the promises God has made to his people in the Bible, some say it is more than three thousand.

Another source says it is over five thousand. Either way, God wants to bless us with good things and answer our prayers.

But sometimes we read and hold on to a promise in God's Word, and he doesn't seem to fulfill it for us. This is often one of the reasons so many are set back or lose their faith altogether. First, let me say this: you can't put God in a box. He is not a one-size-fits-all genie in a bottle. His timing is not our timing. And this next one is a biggie: God doesn't always just fix our problems—he knows the beginning from the end and will do what is the best thing for us, and often we can't see that. Sometimes he just answers us with a "no," but he is still a promise keeper.

When it comes to putting our faith in God and his promises, we must do our part. Many of his promises have two little words in front, "if you," and two more little words following, "then I." In other words, God requires obedience on our part before the promise is released.

In Matthew 6:33 (NIV), Jesus said: "seek first his kingdom and his righteousness, and all these things will be given to you as well." What comes first before we fill in the "all these things"? Seeking him. I think that also helps us understand that if we seek him and his righteousness, we will not be asking for things that are harmful or that will make us boastful or arrogant—fancy cars, lots of money, prestige, etc. We will be seeking God's will!

I think our confidence in God falters and we take a step backward in faith when we pray without first seeking him, when we expect God to move on our behalf. When nothing happens or when the situation gets worse, the waves start crashing against our faith and we start to sink. Instead of putting our confidence in Jesus, trusting that he will do what is best for us and not allow us to drown in the waves, we get sidetracked in demanding the promise.

We often don't think about checking our own hearts to see if we've done our part. God loves us and he is sovereign, so that's where our faith should be anchored. The more we get out of the boat and fix our eyes and trust in Jesus, the greater our faith will increase.

Guess what? We don't always get our way. Think about it. When children are small, does a parent give them everything they ask for just because they cry for it? Candy at bedtime or an expensive toy off the Walmart shelf? Would a good mother give a one-year-old the bottle of milk that was accidently overheated in the microwave just because they screamed for it? I don't think so. Good parents do what is best for their child even though the child doesn't like it or understand it right then. Good parents make good choices for their children until they can make good choices for themselves. God is a good Father, and he does what is best for us, too. We are his children.

If we want to increase our faith and reignite the zeal we once had for God, we should first know that he loves us. We should believe that he cares about every detail of our lives and wants what is best for us. And when he makes a promise to us like this one from Isaiah 40:29–31, we can believe every word:

> He gives power to the weak and strength to the power-
> less. Even youths will become weak and tired, and
> young men will fall in exhaustion. But those who trust
> in the LORD will find new strength. They will soar high
> on wings like eagles. They will run and not grow weary.
> They will walk and not faint. (NLT)

## Walk and Not Faint

That brings us right back to where we started—getting out of the boat and walking on water without fainting or sinking into the storm swirling around us. The "if you" part of that promise in Isaiah 40 is for those who "trust in the Lord." If we are to walk on water without sinking, we must have confidence to trust in the Lord. That means daring to put your faith in him, even though the circumstances look impossible. After all, he is the God of the impossible! His promise goes beyond keeping us from sinking or fainting. The Word says if we trust in the Lord, we will find new strength, even "soar high on wings like eagles." That is the kind of faith I want—I want to soar.

A few years ago, my husband and I faced the possibility of losing our business, which Harvey built from scratch more than thirty years ago. It was truly an "American dream" story. But the economy and a number of other factors were threatening to shut us down. Not only would we lose everything we worked so hard for over the years, but all of our employees would also lose their jobs. There was even a very real threat of losing our home.

We had done all that was humanly possible to turn it around, but the situation was out of our control. Unless God brought a miracle, Clark Industries would be no more. This was a huge storm in our lives. All we could do was look to Jesus.

That is exactly what we did. We saw him through the waves and, like Peter, asked him to bring us out there to walk on the water with him. Getting out of the safety of our boat, we dared to trust him for our good. We prayed night and day, and had several friends praying too. We confessed and repented of some bad decisions we had made, and we asked for the forgiveness and mercy of God.

The most amazing thing both my husband and I noticed as we were facing the very real possibility of losing it all was that we weren't afraid. We had the peace Jesus promised in his Word, a peace that goes beyond our understanding. We didn't want to lose our business, but we had a peace in knowing God would still take care of us if we did. The more we clung to Jesus, the less we feared the loss. Then, the miracle happened. God brought a buyer for that portion of our business at a good price, and the storm was over. It was as if he rebuked the winds and the waves and calmed the storm. The employees kept their jobs, and God worked the situation out for our good.

Is there a limit to God's power? The obvious answer is "no." There is nothing God cannot do. If we are praying as if the problem is bigger than God, Jesus will continue to ask us, "Where is your faith?" I'm not trying to minimize your problems. There is nothing minimal about divorce, death, disease, or losing your business, but God is bigger than any of these, and so is his love for you. If you want Jesus to look at you in the storm and say, "O you of *great* faith," I want to challenge you to get out of the boat and trust him. "Let us draw near with a true heart in full assurance of faith . . ." (Heb. 10:22 KJV).

# Chapter 7

# Enter His Gates

"Enter his gates with thanksgiving and his courts with praise;
  give thanks to him and praise his name."

—Psalms 100:4 NIV

**Today, when most of us** think of gates, we think about an outside door hanging from the fence on some hinges—a way into the backyard. Or if you live in the country like I do, it might be the entrance to your property. My son has a big metal gate at the entrance to his place, but he seldom shuts it because it's just too much trouble to open and close it whenever he comes and goes.

Gates don't hold the same significance for us as they did in biblical times. Ancient cities were built with high walls that encircled them for fortification, and the gates were the only way of passing through the wall. These gates were an important part of most ancient cities. In fact, one could usually find a hub of activity swirling around the city gate. Kings often held court at the city gate, and it is where the elders of the city would be seated. Important business was conducted at the city gate. That's where Boaz made the deal with his kinsman for Naomi and Ruth's redemption.

In this next phase of our pilgrimage to reignite our faith, we'll pass through the king's gates to enter into his courts. The king's gates are the place where we enter into his presence, in his courts. His courts within the gates are a place of mercy, protection, communion, and provision. There we are seated with him, just like the elders who sat at the city gate to conduct their business in ancient days.

To be clear, I'm not talking about the pearly gates we pass through in the sweet by and by after we die. I'm talking about the spiritual gates we pass through in prayer. We may enter as often as we want, at any time, night or day. His gates are always open to us. Jesus made it clear that the kingdom of God is at hand, right now. It is for those who believe and put their trust in him—his friends. The king has invited us, his friends, into his courts to be in his presence. As believers, we are always welcome into his courts—the Lord will never turn us away. However, *how* we enter his gates can directly affect the flame of our faith.

## Our Approach

The Holy of Holies should be approached with reverence. Yes, Scripture does tell us we can enter boldly into the throne room of grace (Heb. 4:16), but this is talking about *access*. There are times we burst through the gates in desperation, in pain or in need of comfort, and our loving God is there with open arms to wrap around us and heal. We have unhindered access to God almighty because of the sacrifice Jesus paid on the cross with his blood for our sins. That alone should put us in a mindset of reverence and gratitude as we enter his gates.

But bursting through his gates with our agenda in hand is not only irreverent, but detrimental to our faith. Why? Because when we are focused on ourselves and our wants, our pain, and our needs, we overlook and miss all the benefits and blessings of being in the presence of God. God wants us to bring our problems to him, but when we enter with praise on our tongue while remembering the goodness of God, our faith to believe in his power is heightened. King David understood this. Take just a moment right now to open your Bible and read through Psalm 103—it's not very long.

Did you notice that in the second verse David reminded himself to never forget all the good things God has done for him? David's faith was fanned into a flame as he made declaration after declaration of the goodness of God.

Entering God's gates with thanksgiving causes us to lay down our agenda and acknowledge and show gratitude for what he has done for us—how he has answered prayers, shown us favor and blessed us, protected us, and more. As we enter his courts with praise, it's hard not to be confident that Jesus will take care of everything concerning us—he delights in giving us the desires of our hearts.

## Friendship

Of all the people I know, I call many of them my friends. Some people have thousands of friends on Facebook, many of whom they've never met. But they wouldn't consider all those friends to be real friends. You may know a lot of people through work, church, activities, and school, but they're not the people you hang out with. These friends are more like acquaintances. Real friends know each other. They know each other's birthdays without Facebook pop-up reminders. You know your real friends' personalities, likes, and dislikes. Close friends share their hearts with each other. That's how Jesus knew his disciples, and that's why he called them friends.

Friends enjoy spending time together. This is how it should be for us when we spend time with Jesus in his courts.

## Twins

Monique Mubiru and I have a close friendship. She is Ugandan. When we met in 1998 on her first trip to the United States, she came to a Bible study I was leading and we instantly connected. We are kindred spirits in our personalities, vision for ministry, and love of Jesus and family. Over the years, our hearts have been knit together, and more than just as sisters in Christ. We, an African and an American, are spiritual twins.

Monique and I live on different continents and grew up in different cultures, but somehow, God brought us together to serve him in partnering ministries. When she needs something, she doesn't give me a long laundry list of needs—I already know what's on her list. The same goes for me. When I have a need, I don't give her a list, either. Our open and constant communication allows us to work together and still concentrate on our friendship. We share our hearts. Sometimes we chat online and share a nugget the Holy Spirit has taught us or about something special going on in our family. Other times, if we're under a lot of stress, we encourage each other. That's what friends do. Our needs are secondary to our friendship. We pray for each other's needs, but the most important things are our relationships with each other and with God. I believe when God calls someone his friend it is because there is a bond and relationship—like the one shared between Monique and me.

## Friend of God

Abraham was called a friend of God (James 2:23). He talked with God as a friend. Jesus called his disciples his friends (John 15:15).

The disciples spent three years traveling, eating, and camping out with Jesus. You can't help but get to know someone well when you spend so much time with him or her. In human terms, we get to know the good, the bad, and the ugly. But because with God there is no bad or ugly, we only get to know his goodness.

When Moses asked God to show him his glory, Scripture says God put him in the protection of the cleft of the rock and his goodness passed before him (Exod. 33:18–19). His goodness is his glory, and his glory is his goodness. When we remember and remind ourselves of God's goodness toward us, our confidence and faith are naturally built up. We have greater faith to know that God cares for us, that he loves us, and that he can handle the "to do" list we came with. We don't have to be worried, concerned, or least of all, frustrated. He's got this.

God revealed all his compassion and grace to Moses, and that is exactly what happens for us when we enter his courts with thanksgiving and praise, and then hang out and spend time with Jesus in his courts and in his presence. God's goodness is revealed in his presence, and in his presence is fullness of joy (Ps. 16:11).

Entering his gates with an agenda in our hand is not only an irreverent way to approach the King of kings, but it disregards the fellowship he wants to have with us while we are with him in his presence.

## African Emails

I don't know if this ever happens to you, but when I'm not getting what God is trying to tell me or if the thing he's trying to teach me goes right over my head, he will use an unconventional method of getting through my thick skull. On one such occasion, God used African emails to teach me about the way I should approach him, or enter his gates. In Psalms 100:4–5, the psalmist could have been writing an African email in the way he approached the Lord:

> Enter his gates with thanksgiving;
>> go into his courts with praise.
>> Give thanks to him and praise his name.
> For the LORD is good.
>> His unfailing love continues forever,
>> and his faithfulness continues to each generation. (NLT)

Because of my work there, I have a lot of friends in Uganda, and we generally communicate by email. Early on, I noticed a stark contrast between the way my Ugandan friends and my American friends communicate with each other. When I get emails from my friend, Monique, or any of my other African friends, they always open with praise to God, followed by some sort of acknowledgement of what he has done and a greeting in the name of Jesus. This greeting is followed by kind words of thanks for my work here in the United States or there in Uganda. After that, they inquire about me, my family, people in our church, or friends we may have asked them to pray for—because they have been praying. My African friend then goes on to tell me what God is doing in their church, with an outreach or at the hospital. It is only after all of this that they finally mention their own needs and specific prayer requests. Convicting.

When I think about all the times I've fired off emails that contain no praise to God or inquiry of how anyone is doing, and that offer just a quick greeting before jumping right into the concerns or business at hand, I have to awe at their love and grace in our friendships. Culturally, I, like many Americans, don't like to waste time or effort. We often like to get right to the point in order to fix whatever problem we're facing, and then check it off the list. This kind of communication can lack warmth, and certainly doesn't nurture relationships.

God brought these African emails to my attention one day when I was stressing over information I had been waiting on. My African friends were not in a hurry. If they say they will get something to you right away, that could mean anything—a day, a week, or a month.

## Nanono Winnie

We received a packet of letters from Ugandan children in our school sponsorship program (a few times a year, all the children in our program write to their sponsors). But one little girl named Nanono Winnie did not send a letter. Normally when this happens, it is because the child was away visiting their family during the holiday break on the day they wrote the letters. That is understandable, but this was her third time to miss.

Winnie's sponsor was a little girl with a twin brother. Her brother had received several letters from his sponsored child, but she hadn't received any from Winnie, except the initial one when they started their sponsorship. The twins' mother contacted us to inquire, because her daughter was very disappointed every time letters came. Ordinarily, we bring it up to Moses Bogere, our sponsorship director in Uganda, and he looks into it. But in this instance, we were anxious to hear back quickly and get a letter via email for the sponsor, so we directly contacted Monique, who heads up the whole program.

More than a week had passed since we requested information and a letter from the girl, and I was getting a little irritated. I knew the twins' mother was waiting to hear back from us, so I was feeling a little pressure. Finally, after my patience was running a little thin, I fired off an email to Monique. My email was typical and hurried: "Hi Monique. I'm still waiting for a letter from Nanono Winnie . . ." Her reply was gracious and filled with detail:

> Praise God, Twin. I greet you in the Almighty Name of Jesus. We saw many salvations in our mission to Gomba. God is doing amazing things. How are you and your family? Please send my greetings to Harvey. How is Pastor Matt? Thank you so much for loving us and for the work you are doing in the sponsorship program. May God bless you . . .

She went on to tell about her family and what God is doing in their ministry. And then finally, "I have not yet been able to reach the family of Nanono Winnie because they live far from here . . ."

Really? That's it? She lives far from there? If she is so far, I thought, then she should have been dropped from the program. Frustrated, I wrote back another short and to-the-point email. That's when the Lord yanked on my chain.

## The Rest of the Story

In Monique's next email, the whole story about this twelve-year-old girl came out. Her parents died, and she had been moved to go and live with her grandmother and uncle, who resided hours away near the equator. They were her only living relatives. Normally in our school sponsorship program, if a child moves outside of our area, they lose their sponsorship because it is too hard to keep up with them. But in Winnie's case, her grandmother and uncle begged Moses not to drop her because they were in such destitute poverty. School was all the hope this little girl had left for a future.

Knowing that the mission of our ministry is to be a reflection of Christ to those we serve, our director chose compassion. Because of distance, Winnie could not participate when the other children wrote letters, but Moses was planning to make a trip to the equator to get one for us. I felt like a heel.

My approach to Monique was short and typical of my hurried American lifestyle. She, in turn, was gracious and had been working on the situation the whole time—typically gracious, as most Ugandans tend to be. The Holy Spirit showed me that I approach the gates of almighty God in much the same way. Instead of going through his gates with thankfulness and entering his courts with hands raised in praise, I barge through his gates and into his presence while waving a to-do list in my hand. Without the slightest acknowledgment of all he has done or nod to what he is doing for me, I'm ready to take my seat at the gate and get right down to business. There is no praise on my tongue or worship in my heart; only frustration because things haven't been happening fast enough or going the way I think they should.

I was humbled when the curtain was pulled back and I got a glimpse of what had been happening "behind the scenes" in Uganda. While I felt bad for our sponsor's little girl who was disappointed at not receiving a letter from Winnie, my heart was broken for Winnie. She'd not only lost her parents, but had also been moved far away from her friends and everything familiar to go live with an elderly grandmother and an uncle.

My friends in Uganda hadn't dropped the ball; all along, they had been compassionately working to help everyone involved, which included Winnie, her sponsor, and me. God doesn't drop the ball, either. We can't always see what is happening behind the scenes, but we can be confident that God is always working compassionately for our good (Rom. 8:28).

## Faith and Praise

After the dust settled with Winnie and her sponsor, the Holy Spirit, in his gentle and loving manner, reminded me that I can and should praise God, regardless of whether I can see what I'm hoping for. This is spelled out in Hebrews 11:1: "Now faith is confidence in what we hope for and assurance about what we do not see" (NIV). A good measure of my weariness is born out of my weakened faith because I am looking at things as they are, not as I am hoping for.

The Holy Spirit broke through my thick skull to reach down into my agenda-minded heart to make me ask myself: If God, through our Ugandan friends, has been working behind the scenes so compassionately for Winnie, what else has he been doing that I don't know about? With that thought in mind, the Holy Spirit began to reignite my faith in God. My entrance into his gates brought a little more humility, thanksgiving, and praise on my tongue. When the Holy Spirit ignites faith in us, we have more confidence—not so much in what we want to see, but in our God. When we have faith, it is easy to praise and worship God, who is worthy of all praise!

## Praise and Worship

There is a term for "entering his gates with thanksgiving and his courts with praise." It's called praise and worship. This is what naturally flows out of a heart set on Jesus and his goodness. Most often, it is manifested in songs of praise.

Singing songs of praise to God is one of the best ways to lift us out of the muddy grubbies and into a right attitude for entering his gates and courts. When I'm not in a good frame of mind, singing praises to God will usually break whatever is holding me back.

While some people are very gifted with beautiful singing voices, there are plenty of people like me who can't carry a tune in a bucket. I'm just glad the Scripture gives us a pass. "Make a joyful noise to the LORD . . ." (Ps. 98:4 ESV).

I like to sing . . . along. I like to sing along with people who sing well, so I can fade into the background where no one can hear me. And that's okay. It's not about talent or singing ability—I'm still worshiping the Lord because my heart is full of praise. I don't usually have a choir around me to help me enter into the presence of God, so I just turn on Christian radio or pull up some praise tunes on my phone. If you don't have a song in your heart, I would encourage you, too, to find some music that will help you enter God's presence. Do it every day, make a habit of entering his gates with an attitude of gratitude, and watch your flame grow.

# Chapter 8

# Digging for Diamonds

"To have found God and still to pursue Him
is the soul's paradox of love."

—A. W. Tozer, *The Pursuit of God*

**After being a follower of** Christ for a while, reading and studying his Word and experiencing a transformed life, I came to the
realization that I was in a place of spiritual satisfaction. Not that
I'd "arrived," but somehow I was comfortable in my faith, and the
desire to pursue more of God and his Word had faded. This is a
dangerous place to be for any Christian. Like sheep comfortably
grazing in a pasture, it is easy to let down our guard, leaving the
gate wide open for the enemy to come in and undermine the power
of God in our lives. Even Jesus likens us to the sheep he loves and
cares for, and he warns us of Satan, whose agenda is that of a thief
looking for opportunities to kill, steal, and destroy (John 10:10–11).

Before I met Jesus, my life had no purpose or hope, and I lived
to please myself. Saved only by the grace of God, I was grateful. So
naturally, as a new believer, Jesus had top billing in every part of
my life. Whenever I saw lost and hurting people, I wanted them to

have what I found in Jesus. It broke my heart if they rejected the gospel, and that motivated me to pray for them.

The Bible was my go-to book. It was nothing for me to spend half the day with Jesus as he walked me through the pages of Scripture. I lived the stories of Solomon asking for wisdom, the widow filling pots with oil that was miraculously provided by God, and Mary sitting at Jesus's feet. I felt Paul's struggle when he said he did the things he didn't want to do and didn't do the things he knew he should. I found myself drinking living water with the Samaritan woman, and identifying with a young queen Esther who chose to rise above her pride to do what was right, no matter the cost. Every day was a new adventure of faith. As I read the words written in the pages of Scripture, God taught, convicted, humbled, encouraged, and empowered me to live my life for him. God carved his heart and will into mine.

## Stagnation

But as the years passed and as I became more familiar with the Christian life, the Bible, and even my relationship with Jesus, something shifted and changed in me. I got bored. Not bored with God, but bored with the Christian routine. Opening my Bible and flipping from one book to another, pausing here and there to read a highlighted passage, I felt stagnant, so I read it less often. And when I did read, it was more out of duty than with open eyes or an open heart.

The definition of "stagnation" is "to be in a rut. Stuck in an established routine, mired in monotony."[1] I know the Word of God is alive, active, and full of treasures, so the problem couldn't have been with the content—it had to have been with me. In all the busyness of my churchy life, I lost interest in mining for treasures in the Bible. Unless the gem was lying out in plain sight and easy to pick up and put into my treasure box, I passed it by.

## Crater of Diamonds

Here in Arkansas, not far from my home, is a state park called Crater of Diamonds, which is visited by over one hundred thousand people every year. It is a 37.5-acre field of volcanic soil. That might be fascinating to some, but on the surface, it just looks like a big field of dirt. But the attraction isn't the dirt—it's what's hidden in the dirt: diamonds. Anyone can pay ten dollars and dig in the dirt to their heart's content. Whatever they find is theirs to keep, even if it's a diamond.

Have I found a sparkling gem at Crater of Diamonds State Park? No. I've yet to put my foot to the first shovel of volcanic soil. In fact, even though this treasure field is less than fifty miles from my home, I've never been there. The thought of spending a day digging in the dirt doesn't really appeal to me, so I don't. But for some people who are willing to take the time and do the work, their efforts have paid off.

In 2015, a lady from Colorado saw Crater of Diamonds State Park on a highway map while visiting nearby Hot Springs and decided to check it out. Her afternoon of digging and sifting paid off. She found an 8.52-carat diamond which was half the size of a quarter.

Diamonds of all sizes have been found by people willing to dig for them. The owner of the 4.25-carat Kahn Canary diamond, also found at the Arkansas site, loaned it to First Lady Hillary Clinton to wear to her husband's presidential inaugural galas in 1993 and 1997 as a special way to represent the state of Arkansas. Stories of amazing finds abound. Children and adults alike have unearthed all sizes of diamonds and other precious stones.

God's Word, like this volcanic crater, is filled with hidden treasures. We know amazing mysteries are hidden within its pages, but the truth of the matter is, we just don't feel like digging. Yes, God can speak to us through prayer, prophesy, and, occasionally, dreams and visions like he did for Daniel and Joseph. But even those must be tested in light of the Scriptures, and that, too, requires a little digging. Most of the time, God speaks to us through his written Word, the Bible. The Bible is God's Word to us. In fact, Jesus *is* the Word (John 1:1–2).

One of Satan's most successful tactics to weaken the church is to pull believers like you and me away from God's Word. Why? Because, Satan knows the value and power of God's Word in a believer's life. The Scriptures are not just sixty-six books bound up in a leather cover; they are the living words of almighty God, and they are as sharp as a double-edged sword. Satan knows he can be defeated by it, so he tries to blind us to its power, distract us from spending time in it, and then bring discouragement—anything to keep us from taking up our sword. This razor-sharp sword in the hand of a believing Christian will penetrate and cut through all the layers of falsehoods, pretenses, and deceptions the enemy tries to set up against the truth. It also brings wisdom, encouragement, comfort, and whatever we might need to face any situation life hands us. Unfortunately, when we lay down our sword and quit seeking God, complacency and stagnation occur, leaving the gate wide open for the enemy who never misses an opportunity to kill, steal, and destroy.

I could write this chapter on techniques and ways to discipline oneself in the study of God's Word, but I feel the Holy Spirit leading me in a different direction. We already know what we need to do—spend time digging in the Word of God. We even know how to do that. We know the times and circumstances that work best for us in our busy lifestyles. Many of us have been reading the Scriptures for years. Instead, I'm asking the Lord to reveal to us the true value of Scripture. Psalms 119:105 describes the Scriptures as a lamp for our feet. It shows us the way to walk, to keep from stumbling and falling over the obstacles in our way.

Going back to the Crater of Diamonds, its 37.5-acre field looks like a vast, dirty field in the middle of nowhere. If you don't recognize the value of its hidden treasures, you're certainly not going to spend an afternoon in the hot Arkansas sun, digging and sifting through the dirt to find one.

The lady who uncovered the 8.52-carat diamond thought she found a piece of quartz crystal—also a common find in Arkansas. She had no idea the real value of what she had unearthed until she took it to the on-site experts, who told her it was the fifth-largest diamond ever discovered in the park since it opened in 1972.

## Making the Cut

There are many angles and ways to cut a raw diamond, and if the diamond cutter knows what he's doing, the resulting stone can be brilliant and stunning in its reflection of light. That is precisely how the words of God in Scripture reflect Jesus in us. God knows exactly what he is doing. He knows how to cut the Word in us to bring about the perfect reflection of himself.

Diamonds in the rough don't really look like much. In fact, it's hard to truly appreciate what you might be holding in your hand when it's in its natural, raw state. But the more you cut into the rock, the more its value is revealed. This can also be said of

Scripture. We don't always understand what the value of a simple verse might have until that verse is read, examined, and dissected.

## A Hidden Gem

For example, during the first years of my marriage to Harvey, I had a hard time adjusting to being a stepmother to his three daughters. I won't go into all the gory details, but because of their loyalty to their mother and things that were said about me to them, our relationship was very strained. I tried hard to walk out my Christian faith, but the onslaught of negative words and actions took their toll. Little by little, resentments and anger built up until I became like a tinderbox. It didn't take much to set me off. One little spark and I'd blow.

I read the verses about turning the other cheek, loving those who spitefully use you, and considering it all joy when you encounter various trials. But to be honest, I was fed up. I complained to God on a daily basis about how unfairly I was being treated and about how my husband seemed to care more about keeping his ex-wife happy than he seemed to care about me.

Then one morning, after blowing a major gasket in an explosive confrontation over a school project, I finally had all I could take. In the aftermath, feeling regret and shame over how I'd acted, I collapsed in surrender at Jesus's feet, totally defeated. If anyone who didn't know me had witnessed the scene that had occurred just an hour earlier, they never would have imagined I was a born-again Christian. I just thank God for his mercies and forgiveness.

In that "come to Jesus" moment, I opened up my Bible. For some reason, I found myself reading in Proverbs 31 about how a godly woman should behave—probably my way of subconsciously beating myself up to feel even worse than I already did. But my eyes rested on verse 26: "She opens her mouth with wisdom, And on her tongue *is* the law of kindness" (NKJV).

It was obvious that wisdom hadn't been flowing out of my mouth when I had opened it, but the thing that grabbed me was how it said *the law* of kindness was on her tongue. What is the law of kindness? I pushed my shovel a little deeper into the soil, and saw the faint glimmer of a hidden treasure—something I'd previously missed or overlooked.

Lifting that raw diamond out of God's Word and holding it up to the light, I really had no idea what it would be worth to me in the coming years. It wasn't until I brought it to the Lord and laid myself at his feet, repentant and open to hear what the Spirit was saying, that he began to cut and shape this gem in me. He began to teach me the law of kindness. Proverbs 15:1 puts it like this: "A gentle answer deflects anger, but harsh words make tempers flare" (NLT). The gentle answer requires exercising kindness. When in the midst of a hostile environment, this is not an easy thing to do. The natural, fleshly response is to react in kind, not in kindness.

The beautiful thing about any natural law is that they always have the same result—they don't change. Take the law of gravity, for example. If you hold a rock in your hand and you let it go, it will fall. It's a law—it happens every time. The rock will always fall down and hit the ground when you let it go. Isaac Newton's law of motion says that an object in motion continues in motion with the same speed and in the same direction unless acted upon by an unbalanced force. If a car is rolling down the road, it will continue to roll until something stops it—the brakes, a wall, or a cliff.

Spiritually speaking, my anger and resentments were rolling down the road at a furious pace until God threw on the brakes with the law of kindness. I'm just glad he kept me from going over the cliff.

I found that actions and words spoken in kindness had the same consistent results as any other biblical principle. Kindness generally defuses wrath. In answer to my cries, God wanted to infuse his brand of kindness into my life as a follower of Christ so I could not only have a better relationship with my stepdaughters, but also be a reflection of God.

I began by putting a guard on my tongue, and looked for ways to respond to my stepdaughters with kindness, despite how they treated me. As I permitted the law of kindness to rule my tongue, the conflicts in our home were greatly diminished. Prayers for my stepchildren began to replace the resentments I had been holding on to, until gradually and steadily, our relationships improved. Today, you cannot tell by looking at our relationships who is my natural child and who is my stepchild. We are all very close.

The value of that "cut diamond" in my life is priceless. It started out in my relationship with my stepdaughters, but the same principle has been just as true in many other situations and circumstances I've encountered with people since then.

The law of kindness is just one very small example of a gem mined from God's treasure field and cut into a glistening reflection of his love. You can probably think of several others that you've uncovered in your walk with God. The fact of the matter is, the diamonds are there, but in our stagnation and disconnect with God, we get tired of digging. We become especially weary with the cutting process, and slip back into the sorts of attitudes and responses we had before we surrendered our lives to Christ.

Being easily offended, getting angry over little things, becoming frustrated with people, feeling discontented with how things are going in our lives, and being generally unhappy are pretty good indicators of how our spiritual flame is burning. And Satan would love nothing more than to keep us in that place. He doesn't want us to uncover the diamonds hidden just below the surface of God's Word. If we do happen to stumble on a gemstone, Satan will do whatever he can to keep it from being cut into our hearts, because as soon as we lift it up to God for the first cut, he loses.

## Growing into Perfection

God doesn't want us to be satisfied with just finding raw diamonds in his Word or with the daily routine of Christian life. He wants us to experience full value, which only comes when we allow him to cut and shape us into a brilliant reflection of himself. That's called growing into perfection. The writer of Hebrews put it this way: "Therefore, leaving the discussion of the elementary *principles* of Christ, let us go on to perfection . . ." (Heb. 6:1 NKJV).

In Philippians 3, the apostle Paul said he had everything to boast about in his accomplishments and education as a Jewish leader, but he considered it all to be trash when compared to gaining perfection in Christ. Paul sought the righteousness that comes by faith in Jesus. He wanted to know Jesus and the power of his resurrection. He knew he wasn't there yet, but he was striving for it, pressing on "so that I may lay hold of that for which also I was laid hold of by Christ Jesus" (Phil. 3:12 NASB). Paul was digging for diamonds, and as quickly as he found them, he handed them over to God to cut them into his life. He wanted to be a reflection of Christ.

The Christians in the Philippian church, like many of us today, believed in Jesus and understood the fundamental truths of the gospel, but they were stuck. Paul knew God had so much more in store for them, and for us too. The wise apostle wrote that in Jesus, "all the treasures of wisdom and knowledge are hidden" (Col. 2:3 TLV).

## Uncut Diamonds

In 2016, while digging alongside her grandmother, a nine-year-old girl from Missouri found a 1.53-carat white diamond at Crater of Diamonds State Park. When questioned about what she would do with this rare gem, young Grace Houston rejected the idea of making it into a necklace. It was also suggested that she could save it for a beautiful engagement ring when she was older and ready to marry. Her reply was, "No! I would never put such a rare and special and precious thing into an expensive piece of jewelry!"[2]

Grace kept her diamond in its natural state, just as she found it. Unfortunately, without cutting, its full potential for beauty will never be realized. That's what happens to us when we settle down into a place of spiritual stagnation, content to understand the basics of our faith in Jesus and happy to keep it that way: "I'm a Christian. I believe in Jesus." This, of course, reminds me of the parable Jesus told about the servant who hid his talents and did nothing with them (Matt. 25:14–30).

If you look back at my experience in uncovering the law of kindness, it's obvious I wasn't out looking for a gem—I just tripped over it, as I was frazzled and at my wits end. This was the case because I had become stagnant in my Christian life, happy with status quo. The gem of kindness was uncovered in my desperation, but the cutting of this gem only began after I took a position of humility and repentance in God's presence, surrendering myself to him. In that moment, with my sin blatantly exposed before a holy God, I had a choice on what I would do with that diamond in the rough (kindness). I could either choose to stick to my guns, anger, and self-justification, and throw it away; or I could humble myself and allow God to do some cutting, pressing on toward perfection.

What Paul was trying to get across to the church in Philippi, and to all of us who read the Word of God, is that if we choose to do some digging, there's no limit to the wealth of treasures available to us in Christ. And if we humble ourselves before a holy God and submit to his cutting, we will see his brilliance shining in our lives. We can grow in perfection without having to wait until we're desperate.

## Fuel for Fire

Like you, I've unearthed some beautiful nuggets of insight and wisdom from God's Word over the years. When I gave God the liberty to cut these truths into my life, I've found they have not only kept me from sinning, but also kept me from making wrong decisions, brought me comfort when I was hurting, gave me victory in impossible situations, and even protected me from making disastrous choices—some of which could have changed the course of my life. If you have been a Christian for any length of time and you've read and applied his Word to your life, I'm certain you know what I'm talking about.

We are on a pilgrimage to get our faith blazing again, and "faith *comes* by hearing, and hearing by the word of God" (Rom. 10:17 NKJV). The intensity of our flame is directly related to the fuel it has to burn. So when we become bored, tired, or burned out in our walk with God, we have to refuel.

By depriving ourselves of this fuel, we not only risk the flame of our faith burning out, but, as I said before, we are also left vulnerable to the enemy. Satan uses our life circumstances, sickness, death, job loss, financial setbacks, and even poor relationships with stepchildren to defeat us. Without a sword in our hand to fight, we can be defeated. That's why so many fall away.

God's Word is like manna, heavenly bread. It is life-giving and sustaining. We need to gather it fresh every day, even if it's just a small portion. But we can't live on yesterday's manna. When we take the time to deliberately read God's Word, even when we don't feel like it, hidden gems will be uncovered. And if we want to see some major changes and victories instead of the status quo, we can hand the gems back to God and give him the freedom to cut away. That's how we grow in perfection and become a reflection of his brilliant light.

## Notes

[1] *Picturesque Expressions: A Thematic Dictionary*, 1st ed., s.v. "stagnation."

[2] "9-Year-Old Missouri Girl Finds 1.53 Carat Diamond in Arkansas," THV11, July 25, 2016, http://www.thv11.com/news/local/9-year-old-missouri-girl-finds-153-carat-diamond-in-ark/280666129.

# Chapter 9

# Turn On the Light!

"We are indeed the light of the world—But
only if our switch is turned on!"

—John Hagee

**Nancy and I are good** friends and ministry partners. We often
room together on our mission trips, and this was one of those
times. We were in India, and let's just say our hotel room was ade-
quate (I'm being polite). But for the sake of illustration, I'll give
you a little more detail.

After traveling across the globe and several time zones, our
hosts picked us up at the airport, drove us to the hotel, and gave us
a few minutes to run in and change our clothes before we jumped
straight into ministry. To say we were experiencing jet lag only
scratches the surface on describing our level of exhaustion. By the
time we got back to the hotel and settled into our room, we were
beyond tired. We couldn't even remember the last shower we'd
had or bed we'd slept in.

After unloading our bags, we looked around the room, and
the first thing to jump out at us was a cobra-shaped bed lamp with

eyes that illuminated when you turned on the light switch. Nice! On the wall, next to the bathroom, was a series of button-type light switches which controlled every light and outlet in the room. When we started pushing these buttons, it was like a mini light show. Fluorescent lights along the walls by the ceiling, over-hanging lights in the center of the room, fans, bathroom light, bathroom fan, cobra eyes, and another table lamp all flashed on and off with these quirky buttons. We got a little chuckle out of the weird setup, but because we were so tired and knew we had a full schedule beginning first thing in the morning, we just wanted to go to bed.

Nancy, a bath person by nature, was thrilled to discover an oversized tub, and said, "There is nothing like a good soak to usher in a good night's sleep." To help herself adjust to the radical time change and jet lag, she took a sleeping pill, enjoyed her bath, and then climbed into bed. After my shower, I switched off the cobra eyes and the overhead light and was out for the night, or so I thought.

Sometime during the night, flashes of light and whirring fans going on and off jolted me awake. There was Nancy, standing in a sleeping-pill stupor with her flashlight pointed at the wall, punch-ing buttons, on, off, on, off, on, off, trying to find the bathroom light, all the while mumbling under her breath (along with a few other unintelligible words): "Turn . . . on . . . the . . . light!" She knew the bathroom switch was there, but she just couldn't find the right one—hence the light show.

Seeing she wasn't in a mood for discussion or instruction on which button controlled the different lights, I retrieved my eyeliner pencil from my makeup bag and proceeded to label the buttons while she was in the bathroom. When Nancy came out, I showed her the labels, and the frustration disappeared from her face. We both went back to bed, and for the rest of that week, we never had another issue with the lights—with the exception of the cobra lamp. Its blue eyes were so creepy that we unplugged it and put it out of sight.

## Pushing Buttons

Christians who experience a kind of stagnation in their faith, even those whose flame is nearly burnt out, can probably relate to Nancy's sleepy, button-pushing frustration. They may be tired of being told to try this or that formula or to read certain books and articles. They may be tired of listening to podcasts and preachers telling them to pray and read the Bible more or to do this study or that one to reignite their faith. Some say to seek God early, others say seek him late, and others say to fast or give of your time and money. But all the while, frustration builds because what they really need and want seems to be eluding them. They know the right button is there, but they just keep missing it and can't find a connection to turn on the light.

## Darkness and Light

If this frustration isn't enough, the world we are living in seems to be growing darker and darker. With this darkness encroaching on the world, blatant sin has become accepted as normal behavior, and many Christians have felt demonized for not embracing it. Our children are inundated with entertainment that's filled with violence, sarcasm, and disrespect for those in authority; and they face intense social pressure and possible persecution if they don't accept these attitudes and behaviors as normal and acceptable— even when they are clearly called sin in the Bible.

I used to listen to the news religiously to stay on top of what was happening in the world around me, but lately, I've found myself going days without turning it on. Every day there is some sort of senseless shooting or attack on innocent people, all motivated by hatred. Darkness seems to be penetrating the world more deeply every day.

While all of this is going on around us, we who call ourselves followers of Christ continue to try and walk out our faith while facing our own daily challenges with family, work, ministry, health, finances, and more. Is it any wonder we see our spiritual flames burning low?

What do we do? What is the answer? How do we reconcile everything in the world and in our lives with our faith in Jesus Christ? How do we turn on the light? Lord, will you please make sense of this crazy world we're living in?

## Lamplight

Early on in my own pilgrimage to reignite my smoldering wick, the Lord gave me a simple word in response to this prayer. Even though I was doing mission work, speaking, and writing, I felt really discouraged, dry, and distant from God because of all the things I just mentioned. I prayed simply, "Lord, open your Word to me and reignite my faith." The prayer was nothing profound—in fact, it felt like my plea just left my lips, traveled upward, hit the ceiling, and fell right back down into my lap. But when it did, a single word came to my mind: "lamp."

I thought about all the places in Scripture that lamps are mentioned, and how they are connected somehow to the spirit of man and the presence of God. Curious as to what the common lamp looked like in biblical times, I did an online search. I expected to see pictures of golden lamps like the one in the story of Aladdin, but what I found instead were pictures of small, hand-formed clay bowls with a spout at one side. They were usually small enough to fit into the palm of the hand so they could be carried from room to room. The descriptions said the lamps were filled with olive oil, and had a strip of woven flax laid into the bowl as a wick. One end of the flax came out of the spout and drew oil up from the bowl to the surface, where it was lit.

Looking at those little lamps and thinking about the parables that include lamps, I became even more curious about their significance in the Bible as they relate to spiritual health. Because I had tried fanning my flame with Bible studies at home and all the other things I mentioned earlier, I decided to do a study on the biblical use of the word "lamp."

In both the Old and New Testaments, there are numerous places that talk about lamps in a spiritual sense. The Word of God is described as a lamp to our feet. David's men described him as the lamp of God in Israel. Ten virgins waiting for the groom had lamps. The woman who lost one of her ten coins lit a lamp. Jesus walked between the seven lampstands. Jesus told people at the church in Ephesus that they'd lost their first love and that he would put out their lamp if they didn't repent. There are several other references, but these are just a few that got my attention.

Because I am a hands-on kind of person, I wanted to see how these small clay lamps worked. So I bought some modeling clay to make my own lamp. After shaping it like the ones described online and hardening it by baking it in the oven, I took some olive oil from my kitchen cabinet and filled the bowl. I didn't have any flax, so I tore strips off a terry cloth washcloth and laid one end in the oil and the other out of the spout. Then, for the moment of truth, I lit it. It burned perfectly.

Just as in biblical times, I didn't use electricity. My little clay lamp provided enough light for illumination, so I could easily find my way from one dark room to another. I let it burn for a while, but eventually the wick began to put off some black smoke. Then the flame grew dim and nearly went out. There was plenty of oil in the lamp, but the wick had burned down to the point that it became charred and black. It needed to be trimmed. I got a pair of scissors, pulled the wick out a little more, and cut off the burnt part. After relighting the wick, the light burned brightly again. This helped me understand why the ten virgins trimmed their lamps when they woke from their sleep (Matt. 25:7).

I thought about the simplicity of this little clay lamp, with the sole purpose of bringing light. But in order for this lamp to fulfill the purpose for which it was created, four things had to come together. This is when the Holy Spirit began to show me how, in a spiritual sense, we are each like clay lamps. I was about to push the button to turn on the light.

## The Four Elements of the Lamp

God began to reveal to me how we, his people, are like these little clay lamps. In order for us to fulfill the purpose for which we were created, four things must be in place. Without all four elements of the lamp working together, there would be no light to push against the darkness closing in around us. The light within us is the answer—not just so we can burn for Jesus, but also for those living in darkness to find their way to God. Jesus put it this way: "Nor do men light a lamp and put it under a bushel, but on a stand, and it gives light to all in the house" (Matt. 5:15 RSV).

## Clay

The clay vessel is the first and most obvious part of the lamp. We are like clay vessels or containers; and in fact, there are Scriptures describing us as such (Isa. 64:8, 45:9; 2 Cor. 4:7; Jer. 18:4). God, the potter, molds us into containers to be used for his purpose, which is to bring light into a dark world. Each clay lamp, because it is individually created by the potter, looks a little different than the others—no two are exactly alike. We are fearfully and wonderfully made.

It is God the Father who shapes our lives. We belong to him, and he created us to bring his light into a dark world. We get that. But sometimes we forget that we are made from the dust of the earth. We are simply clay containers.

Clay is formed from earth and water. The water added to the earth makes it pliable in the potter's hand. "O LORD, You are our Father, We are the clay, and You are our potter; And all of us are the work of Your hand" (Isa. 64:8 NASB). Without water, the potter can do nothing to shape it into a vessel for his use—in this case, a lamp. The Samaritan woman discovered living water when she met Jesus. It changed who she was, and she became a light for God. The same thing happens to us when we drink of that same living well.

Once the potter forms the clay into a lamp, it must be fired. He has to turn up the heat and let it harden to permanently maintain its shape. None of us like it when the heat is turned up too high. We want to be comfortable, so the first thing we do is crank up the air-conditioning. But when God is in the firing process, there isn't any thermostat to adjust. Enduring the heat and passing through the fire is what makes us strong enough to carry out God's purposes. It is never easy, but the fire is what prepares us for the potter's use. Otherwise, we would fall apart at the first sign of pressure.

## *Oil*

The second element is the oil. Biblically, oil represents the Holy Spirit. Because we are followers of Christ, the Holy Spirit resides in us; gives us wisdom, strength, and power; and provides the fuel we need to meet any and every challenge. Numerous Scriptures attest to this, my favorite being Romans 8:11, which says: "And if the Spirit of him who raised Jesus from the dead is living in you, he who raised Christ from the dead will also give life to your mortal bodies because of his Spirit who lives in you (NIV).

The Holy Spirit takes up residence in us at the moment we first believe and accept Jesus's sacrifice on the cross for our sins. "Don't you realize that your body is the temple of the Holy Spirit, who lives in you and was given to you by God?" (1 Cor. 6:19 NLT).

Obviously, for any lamp to bring light, it must have a fuel supply. But fuel supplies can and do run down, especially when our lives are filled with work, family, stress, health issues, etc. If we allow ourselves to be depleted of the precious fuel of the Holy Spirit, we become dry and useless as a lamp.

Jesus promised to never leave or forsake us, and that is a promise we can hang our hats on. But when we fill our lives with busyness and distractions (yes, even Christian ministries) and forget about the fuel that keeps us going, our oil runs low and our flame is at risk of going out. This can happen without us even realizing it, especially when we're busy doing God's work. Low fuel must be replenished. It is critical that we strengthen ourselves in the Lord by carving out and guarding time for him.

Jesus's parable of the ten virgins (Matt. 25:1–13) immediately comes to mind when I think about our oil running low. All ten young women knew the groom was coming, but while the groom was delayed, they fell asleep. This is where many are today in the church: sleeping while we wait for Jesus's return. In the parable, when the groom finally did come, five of the women were prepared with plenty of oil to refuel their lamps, and the other five were not. The five who had allowed their lamps to run out of fuel missed God. They were left behind while they scrambled to find more oil. Jesus is right at the door, and we might hear the sound of the trumpet at any time. The time to refuel is before he comes.

The Holy Spirit is the third person of the Trinity. He is not a commodity or something that's dished out as we pray here and do a good deed there, like payment for a job well done. The Holy Spirit isn't a ghost, though he is often referred to as the Holy Ghost. The Holy Spirit is God—God's presence living in each one of us. He is the power of God. He is a comforter and helper. He gives us wisdom, knowledge, and counsel. He is a friend in time of need, but the Holy Spirit can also be grieved. It is the Holy Spirit of God that leads us into all truth. If we want to see God's will on earth as it is in heaven, we will maintain a fresh supply of this amazing oil in our lamps.

## The Wick

The third element is the wick, which represents our faith—the conduit through which the Holy Spirit within us is drawn out (Mark 11:24; Heb. 11:1; 1 Pet. 1:8–9; 1 John 5:4). "And without faith it is impossible to please God, because anyone who comes to him must believe that he exists and that he rewards those who earnestly seek him" (Heb. 11:6 NIV). The wick is kind of a tricky element of the lamp, because it requires maintenance. After it burns for a while, it must be trimmed.

The wick, like our faith, soaks up treasure and then acts as a conduit for the Spirit. After we've been burning for a while, our faith can become charred. Even though our spiritual wicks are soaked with revelation and knowledge of the Scriptures, they must be trimmed regularly of disappointments, failures, sins, and offenses for the Spirit to flow and maintain a steady flame.

The Holy Spirit cannot continue to flow through us if we don't periodically examine our hearts and cut away any sin or unforgiveness. If we hold onto offenses, refusing to let go and forgive, not only is the flow of the Holy Spirit stopped, but his Word says he will not even listen (Ps. 66:18). The only way to trim our wick is to repent. Even Jesus said: "So if your hand or foot causes you to sin, cut it off and throw it away. It's better to enter eternal life with only one hand or one foot than to be thrown into eternal fire with both of your hands and feet" (Matt. 18:8 NLT).

As we continue on this pilgrimage, if the Holy Spirit taps you on the shoulder to show you a charred place where your faith is smoldering, stop right then, get out the scissors, and trim it away. How? Ask the Holy Spirit to reveal any hidden sin, unforgiveness, bitterness, or pride. When he does, repent and humble yourself before a holy and righteous God who loves you and is cheering you on. He is ready to embrace you, meet your needs, and lift you up.

My friend asked me, "If the wick is your faith, what does that have to do with forgiving someone?" I told her that if we can't trust God with our lives and hearts enough to forgive someone who has wronged us, no matter how bad it may have been, then we have no faith in him. From the cross, gasping for breath and in unspeakable pain, Jesus said, "Father, forgive them . . ." (Luke 23:34 NIV). We must take up our crosses and follow him. In the same way, we must repent of all bitterness, pride, and sin of any kind.

It is only after that old dead wick is trimmed that our faith can fully carry out the work of the Holy Spirit and bring light into a dark world.

## Fire

And finally, there must be fire. We can have all three elements—the clay vessel, the oil, and the wick—but without fire, the purpose of bringing light cannot be fulfilled. Only God can ignite the fire, bringing all four elements of the lamp together to fulfill its purpose.

The fire of God ignites when we make the connection by praying in faith and believing that he is here and he hears us, loves us, and cares about the things that concern us. When that faith is present, it can freely draw from the Holy Spirit residing within us right up to the surface of this world where we live. That's when fire sparks, power is released, and prayers are answered. A literal example is when Elijah prayed and fire fell from heaven, consuming the water-soaked sacrifice on the altar. This same power is in us.

The key to the fire of God falling and reigniting our faith is in bringing all the elements of the lamp together. But when one or more elements are missing or are not in right standing, the flow is interrupted and the fire cannot burn. The result is weakened faith, discouragement, burnout, unanswered prayers, and spiritual vulnerability.

If you feel like you are spinning your spiritual wheels and going nowhere fast, take some time to examine your lamp. Check for cracks in the clay. If you find any, Jesus is an amazing healer. He knows how to bind up the brokenhearted and pour soothing oil on our wounds. If your oil is running low, all you have to do is ask for wisdom and God will liberally pour out his Spirit. If your faith is weak, trim off the charred places by not hanging on to the past. Cut away anything that stands between you and your fire. Then stand back and watch God ignite your faith again so you can burn brightly for him. One of my favorite Scriptures is Isaiah 42:3, which

Jesus even quoted in Matthew: "A bruised reed he will not break, and a smoldering wick he will not snuff out . . ." (Matt. 12:20 NIV).

God keeps our lamps burning, just as it says in Psalms 18:28: "You, LORD, keep my lamp burning; my God turns my darkness into light" (NIV). We are just vessels, the Holy Spirit in us is the power or the fuel, and our faith is the conduit. When all three come together, the fourth element, the fire of God, comes to ignite the wick and his light shines through us like a lamp. We become the light of the world as Jesus said: "You are the light of the world— like a city on a hilltop that cannot be hidden. No one lights a lamp and then puts it under a basket. Instead, a lamp is placed on a stand, where it gives light to everyone in the house" (Matt. 5:14–15 NLT).

# Chapter 10

# Shaped for a Purpose

"For we are God's handiwork,
created in Christ Jesus to do good works,
which God prepared in advance for us to do."

—Ephesians 2:10 NIV

**It is important that we** see ourselves in the light of the lamp. No matter how long we have believed in Jesus, we're still like a lamp—a fragile clay vessel, shaped for a purpose—not our own, but God's. That purpose is to bring light to the world. Much of the light we bring comes by way of doing good works—works God prepared in advance for us to do, just like it says in Ephesians 2:10. God has a plan for our lives. That plan and the works we do may look different in each of our lives; but whatever it is that we do, it involves pouring our lives and hearts into helping people as an extension of our love for God. We are his hands and feet on this earth.

We can often measure the intensity of our spiritual flame by looking at our works and, more particularly, the motivation behind them. Since the beginning of Christianity, Christians all over the world have been busy fulfilling the purposes of God: sharing the gospel, feeding the poor, and encouraging and helping people. Compassion is the heart of God. Now, let's go back to my whole point in writing this book: fanning the flame and reigniting our faith in God. When we lose our compassion, our zeal for God goes with it. The opposite is also true. When we lose our zeal for God, our compassion goes with it. That doesn't mean we've stopped loving God or believing in him, but the kingdom work (the things we do for God) that we involve ourselves in and our compassion for people suffers. We continue doing what we've always done for God, but for the wrong reasons. This is a trap and snare set up for us by our enemy, the devil.

## Right Thing, Wrong Reason

What you're doing may be right in line with God's will, bearing bushels of spiritual fruit, but perhaps your motivation is a little off center. I recently read a book by Peter Greer, CEO of HOPE International, titled *The Spiritual Danger of Doing Good*. Greer speaks very transparently about a time he was in Rwanda on a mission to hand out blankets to refugees from Ghana who had fled because of a volcano that had consumed their homes. These were devastated people who had lost everything. Greer was up on a platform with people lined up in front of him to receive their blankets. Seeing a photographer, he flashed a cheesy smile for the camera while handing out the blankets. Later, he reflected on that picture by saying:

> Noble cause. Noble mission. Noble actions of a
> twenty-five-year-old relief worker. . . . I smiled wide for
> the camera as I did 'God's work'. . . . Captured on film,
> I recognized myself as playacting for people far away,

not thinking about loving the people in front of me. I thought, I can't wait until the people back home see these photos of me.[1]

"God's work" does indeed need to be done. Because we love God, we are all about doing his work. It is easy to get wrapped up in it: counseling people with addictions, visiting the forgotten elderly in nursing homes, digging water wells in Africa, feeding the hungry, organizing relief for flood or tornado victims, taking care of widows and orphans, or a million other projects. All these "works" are good, but if we forget about the people we are helping, we've missed the point—we just feel good about what we are doing and about ourselves.

God is relational and he loves people, so as Christians, the biggest part of any work he calls us to do involves loving people. God is looking for a heart or spirit that is broken, repentant, and surrendered to him. King David put it this way in Psalms 51:17: "The sacrifice pleasing to God is a broken spirit. God, You will not despise a broken and humbled heart" (HCSB).

When our spiritual flame is ignited by our faith, amazing things happen. God is in the middle of whatever we set our hands to do, and people are drawn to him as a result. He gets all the glory.

I'll never forget how my heart felt the first time I saw a little African girl playing in a mud puddle in the street by our clinic in Uganda. She was about six or seven years old. Most of the children in the area were in school, so I thought it odd that she was playing alone in the street. When I asked why she wasn't in school, I was told she was an orphan who lived with her grandmother, who couldn't pay the school fees.

My heart was full of compassion for that child. At that point in time, I wasn't thinking about starting a school sponsorship program in Uganda; I was just thinking about the destitute life that little girl was certain to have without an education. I felt Jesus's compassion for her, and that compassion motivated me to answer God's call to do something.

Fast-forward fifteen years. As a result of seeing children like that little girl, hundreds of children now attend school and have graduated through our child education sponsorship program. How? God had a plan long before I ever traveled to Africa. He put that little girl along my path, and then used my love for him and my compassion for children to stir up something in me. When I stepped out in faith, he jumped in with his grace, provision, power, and guidance. It wasn't about me or anything I did—God did it all. I was just a vehicle.

But now I ask myself, is compassion still the motivation for my work? I must be honest and say that most of the time, I still have compassion for the children, but there are times that I don't. When the nuts and bolts of the program wear me down, it's easy to lose sight of the children and slip into a state of apathy, treating it like a nine-to-five job. But worse than those moments of apathy are the times when there's a lot of back-patting going on, and I have to put a check on my pride.

## Pat Me on the Back

Whenever we accomplish something good and someone takes note, gushing out compliments and gratitude, buttons start popping off the shirt stretched across our puffed-up chest.

Remember King Nebuchadnezzar? He was the greatest king of ancient Babylon. One day, while strutting around the roof of his palace looking over the splendid city, he nearly broke his arm trying to pat himself on the back. He said to himself, "Look at this great city of Babylon! By my own mighty power, I have built this beautiful city as my royal residence to display my majestic splendor" (Dan. 4:30 NLT). Unfortunately, it didn't go well for the braggadocious Babylonian king, because God had warned him before about his pride, and judgment fell. For the next seven years, King Nebuchadnezzar lost it all, along with his sanity. He ate grass and crawled around like an animal. God humbled him until he acknowledged and gave glory to the Lord for his great accomplishments.

Once King Nebuchadnezzar came to his senses, he did give God all the glory, and everything was restored to him. After that, he honored God, and when reflecting on this experience, he said, "those who walk in pride he is able to humble" (Dan. 4:37 NIV).

Pride is a snare, carefully laid out for us by the enemy and located anywhere God calls us to do his work—it doesn't matter how great or small that work might be. Whether building kingdoms, visiting the sick in the hospital, fixing a widow's plumbing, or handing out blankets to refugees in Africa, if Satan can get us to step into the snare of pride, he'll yank that rope so fast we'll never know what hit us. Once our foundational footings of love and compassion are gone, the tables are easily turned and, suddenly, the work becomes all about you and me. When this happens, any work we do in God's name becomes more about how good we look, how smart we are, how much we've accomplished, how many we've helped, and so on.

Jesus described the religious leaders and their pride like this: "Everything they do is for show. On their arms they wear extra wide prayer boxes with Scripture verses inside, and they wear robes with extra long tassels" (Matt. 23:5 NLT). Looking godly took precedence over being godly. Godliness is being godlike, and to be godlike is to have love and compassion for people.

## God's Economy

In God's economy, the value of what we do for him isn't in how much time or money we spend, or even in how many people we touch or feed. Worth is measured in the love and compassion that move us to do those things.

Think about Jesus's conversation with the disciples as they watched people dropping coins into the offering box at the synagogue. The rich came along and put in large amounts of money, but Jesus called their attention to a poor widow who gave just two copper coins worth only a few cents. He told the disciples she put more into the treasury than the others, because they all gave out of their wealth, but she gave all she had to live on (Mark 12:41–44). The widow's love for God was her motivation.

The most important thing, as well as our first priority and motivation for whatever work we are doing, should be our love for God. The second is love and compassion for people. These two things are our measuring stick. Pride causes us to lose whatever reward we might have gained for eternity, but that's just loss of reward. The greater loss is our relationship with God, because pride is sin and sin separates us from God. Separation from God is Satan's ultimate goal for us. "The LORD detests the proud" (Prov. 16:5 NLT).

My point in saying all of this is not to slap you on the hand and guilt-trip you if you've ever felt good about something you've done for the kingdom. We are all human beings, and yes, we do feel good about helping people. There is nothing wrong with that. If it pleases God, we should be pleased, too. But if we find ourselves burning out or resenting the work we are doing for God, or if we sense a loss of compassion for people, we should pause and pray as David prayed: "Search me, O God . . ." (Ps. 139:23 NKJV). This is all part of reigniting and rekindling our faith in God, and regaining our zeal and compassion for his people.

Now is the time to open ourselves up to be examined by the Holy Spirit. If God convicts us of pride, as he did for Peter Greer, repent. If we've just gotten off track by focusing more on the work than the reason and the heart behind the work, it's time to ask God to bring us back to center, even if that means taking a break from it for a while.

## Oops! I Think I Missed God!

In talking about the good works we do for God, pride can manifest itself in other ways as well. It might not be in patting oneself on the back or basking in the accolades of others; it sometimes can be a little more subtle, like running ahead of God and busying ourselves with good works he never planned for us to do. Can I see a show of hands?

Sometimes I just miss God. By that, I mean I miss his will for me—I get it wrong. I think we all do from time to time. When I miss God, I'm usually completely ignorant of my error, especially while I'm smack-dab in the middle of whatever it is I'm doing "for him". Then, after all is said and done, I'm left wondering why things didn't go as planned, or why God didn't show up like I expected him to.

I can tell you for certain, though, that the problem wasn't God not hearing or answering my prayers. No, it was more likely that I hadn't sought him in prayer. Or if I did seek him, I wasn't listening to what he was trying to tell me, or that I didn't bother waiting for his answer before I just went ahead and did what I wanted to do.

Proverbs 16:3 says, "Commit to the LORD whatever you do, and he will establish your plans" (NIV). In our thinking, that passage sometimes gets a little skewed, because we expect God to bless our plans without truly committing them to him.

We may not have a blatant sin to confess, but it is still important to spend time in prayer to replenish our oil supply. I think the hardest thing for most of us, especially those of us who might consider ourselves "seasoned" Christians, is when we are sincerely doing what we consider the work of God and fail. But failure happens when we don't take time to seek the Lord or examine our own hearts. David prayed for God to search him to see if he had any wickedness. (Ps. 139:23–24). We need to do the same.

If we aren't surrendered to Christ, even though the work we want to do is good, we can find ourselves acting alone—only to fall flat on our faces. Then when things don't turn out like we want, it's easy for the enemy to swoop right in and point his accusing finger. We start blaming others or ourselves, and/or we get mad at God. This opens the door for discouragement to set in, making us want to throw in the towel.

## My Will Be Done

I'm titling this section "My Will Be Done" because during one of my mission trips to Africa, I convinced myself that my will was God's will. I would get the work done, and I would fully expect God to bless it.

That particular year, a lot was going on and everything was happening at lightning speed. In addition to all the normal ministry projects and family matters, I also had to make a decision about two mission trip opportunities. All of it was weighing pretty heavily on my mind. But I'm a "fix it" kind of person, and when under pressure, I have a tendency to just do what needs to be done, check it off my list, and move on.

For several months, I had been praying about a mission to China where I would be speaking in a conference as part of a team. While preparing what I would be speaking, the content flowed easily, and I sensed the Holy Spirit's guidance as I studied the Scriptures. Not only did my preparation come together with little effort on my part, but so did the provision for my airfare and other expenses. There was no doubt in my mind that God opened that door and was ushering me through it to shine a light for him in that nation.

The trip to China was set; but at the same time, I had also been talking with a missionary in Mombasa, Kenya, who had a similar medical center to the one my ministry is building in Uganda. This missionary also worked with an orphanage and school where they grew their own produce to feed the children. I could see from our email conversations and the pictures she sent that their medical center, orphanage, and school were exactly the model we had been praying for in our own Ray of Hope Medical Center and our future orphanage and school.

When this lady invited me to come to Kenya to visit their facilities in the fall while she was there, my spirit leapt. She offered to introduce me to the man who built the facilities, and I believed this would be a valuable connection for the work I was doing in Uganda.

I knew it would put a lot on my plate to take two international trips back-to-back, especially right before the holidays, but I was excited to see her facilities and talk with her about how they did it. Because Uganda is only a quick one-hour flight from Kenya, I figured I could include a short visit with my ministry partners,

John and Monique Mubiru, and share what I learned before heading back to the United States. I would even be home in time for Christmas! Setting my plan in motion, I purchased my ticket and checked that off my list.

As the year progressed and my mission to China drew near, it occurred to me that I would only have one week between my trips to China and Africa. And Thanksgiving happened to fall in that week. Complicating matters even further, my dad was making plans to visit for Christmas, and would be arriving only a few days after I got back from Africa, leaving little time to prepare the house, shop for Christmas, decorate, and prepare meals. (Did I mention that I do all the cooking in my home every holiday for a huge family of twenty-three?)

## Best-Laid Plans

You can probably see where I'm going with this, but I'll go ahead and fill you in on how my best-laid plans unfolded. Before leaving for China, my Thanksgiving menu was set and the turkey was in the freezer. I had done most of my Christmas shopping, and the presents were wrapped. Since I only had Thanksgiving week at home after I returned from China, I planned to get my tree up and the house decorated the day after Thanksgiving, before leaving for Africa so I'd be ready for my dad's arrival when I got back.

Everything was going along as planned. The mission to China was amazing. We immediately heard reports of hearts being touched and encouraged. When I got home, we had a great time with family over a delicious Thanksgiving dinner. The next day, everyone in the family jumped in to help with setting up the tree and decorating the house. I did the final touches on my holiday preparations and started packing for the trip to Africa. And that's when it all started to unravel.

I'd made several similar trips to Africa before, but for some reason, something didn't feel right about this one. On the day that I was to depart, I kept running into obstacles. I slept in and was late getting the final items into my bag. By the time we got out the door, I was frazzled. We raced to get to the airport, but realized there was no way to make the flight. Checking the airline, I found a later flight that would still allow me to make my international connection. I was relieved, but only for the moment. In my packing frenzy, I left all my medications sitting on the bathroom counter. Knowing better than to leave the country without my meds, I had no choice but to rebook another flight for the following day.

I lost a day, but the flight to Kenya was smooth, and my tour of the facilities in Mombasa went well. I hopped on the plane for the short flight to Uganda, excited to see my friends and tell them all about my visit. But when I arrived, no one was there to pick me up. Two hours passed before they finally showed up, apologetically explaining how the van had broken down on the way.

After spending a few days with my friends, I headed home. Even though I had accomplished all my plans, somehow I felt deflated and exhausted. On the return flight, I kept hearing reports of a terrible snowstorm in Europe. This resulted in an extended eight-hour layover at the Nairobi airport. When I finally made it to Paris, there were no flights back to the United States. The snowstorm caused cancellations of most flights in and out of Europe, so I had to find a hotel room.

Normally, I would say being stuck in Paris at Christmastime would be a good thing, but I was dressed for the equatorial African heat. Sleeveless shirts and sandals aren't the best attire for snow, and I was in a hurry to get home before my dad's arrival from California. The entire trip was riddled with obstacles and delays. And to make matters worse, without a coat in Paris, I also picked up a cold. Barely making it back to Arkansas ahead of my father and then jumping right into the holidays, I had to wonder if it was all worthwhile.

Once the holidays were over and we got my dad back to California, I spent some time alone with God to ask him what happened. I complained that Satan gave me nothing but problems from the time I left for Africa until the day I returned. I cried out to the Lord and asked him why he would allow this to happen. Why did he send me to Africa during the holidays and then put me through all of that trouble? This included the added expense of flight juggling and a hotel stay in Paris, and then not even having anything to show for it. From the trip to Kenya and Uganda, I could see there was absolutely no fruit—not one lousy grape. The missionary woman I visited dropped off the radar, and I never heard any more from her.

Once I quit my ranting and whining and actually started listening to God, I'm almost embarrassed to share with you what I clearly heard him say to my spirit. In his still, quiet voice, he said, "I didn't send you. Adding on that trip was your idea, not mine." I knew he was right.

As I said in the previous chapter, the purpose of a lamp is to bring light to a dark world. When God sent me to China, his purpose was fulfilled. But the add-on trip to Africa was just that, an add-on. Going to Africa was my will, and I had my own agenda. God gave me plenty of red flags, but I chose to ignore them. He let me have my way, but it wasn't blessed. As a result, I had all sorts of problems. I made myself open and vulnerable to the enemy's attack, and the effort bore no fruit. The wick of my faith was still burning, but it was charred. Charred wicks produce a lot of smoke, but very little light. Left unchecked, the wick will burn out.

## Note

[1]Peter Greer with Anna Haggard, *The Spiritual Danger of Doing Good* (Bloomington, MN: Bethany House, 2013), 23.

# Chapter 11

# Weary in Well-Doing

"Let us not lose heart in doing good,
for in due time we will reap if we do not grow weary."

—Galatians 6:9 NASB

**Have you become a bit** weary in your well-doing? As I said earlier, for Christians who take commitment to Jesus seriously, it is a way of life that affects everything we do. Because we are talking about burnout, I have to wonder if some of our well-doing might be sucking the oxygen out of our spiritual flames.

In my own life, my ministry work consumes a huge chunk of my time. I love what I do, but to be perfectly honest, there are days I just don't want to hear about *another* need in Africa or write another blog post. That may sound a little callous, but I'm just being honest. Sometimes, I just want to do nothing at all and be responsible to no one—maybe even watch a good movie or do something unheard of, like take a nap in the middle of the day.

## The Burden of Ministry

Whether or not you are in ministry, the burden of ministering to others is on those of us who consider ourselves Christ followers.

Jesus commissioned us to go out into the world and make disciples. We are his hands and feet on the earth. We start out well in well-doing, but in time, something happens.

Some see the work to be their own instead of God's. Sometimes pride rears its head, and the work and people being served become secondary to the recognition or glory gained in service—they find themselves building up their own kingdom instead of God's. Some pour their life and soul into helping people, and become weary of the long hours and the thankless nature of their work. I've talked with missionaries who work with other missionaries, but have no relationship with them outside of ministry. They feel isolated, depressed, and alone.

Others get fed up with the constant needs and demands on their personal time and the sacrifice their families have to make, especially if the people they are trying to help seem ungrateful and act like the missionaries owe the service to them. I think the old saying "20 percent of the people do 80 percent of the work" holds true, especially in Christian service. Serving God can definitely be draining and all-consuming.

Then there are those who come against us and the work God has called us to do. Think about the prophet Elijah, who did some amazing works in the name of God. One of his most notable miracles was when he gathered all of Israel to a mountain for a contest to determine once and for all who the *real* god was: Baal or the God of Israel. The rules were simple enough—set up an altar with an animal sacrifice, and the god who sends fire down from heaven to burn it up is the real god.

The pagan priests danced and cut themselves all day and into the evening without a peep from their god, Baal. After taunting them for a while, Elijah stepped up to the plate. He wasn't satisfied to just lay out a sacrifice, so he soaked it down with water until it spilled over into the ditch he dug around it. Without any hesitation or fear at all, and with everyone looking on, this prophet of God called down fire from heaven and, zap!, the fire fell, the sacrifice was consumed, and all the water was licked up in an instant—an amazing demonstration of the power of the one true, living God. As if that weren't enough, this man of faith took down all the priests of Baal, a bold step in ridding the land of its idolatry. Acting on the Word of God, Elijah was fearless and full of faith and power in service to his God.

And then the tide turned—Queen Jezebel heard about what had transpired. She wasn't happy, and she made a vow to kill Elijah. How did he respond to her death threats? Did he act in faith and power? Did he call fire down to consume her? No, he ran for the hills—depressed, defeated, alone, and hiding in the wilderness. What happened?

Satan came in like a flood to rob Elijah of his victory dance. But before we judge him too harshly, we must admit that we've fallen into the same trap and have also been robbed of our victory dances. It's easy to dismiss our defeats to Satan's wiles, but I think it would profit us to look a little deeper.

## Dividing Soul and Spirit

There is a fascinating passage in Hebrews 4:12 that identifies the cutting-edge power and life of God's Word and how it affects our thoughts, attitudes, and ultimately, our actions. It reads, "For the word of God is alive and active. Sharper than any double-edged sword, it penetrates even to dividing soul and spirit, joints and marrow; it judges the thoughts and attitudes of the heart" (NIV).

Though they are often thought of as one and the same, there is a distinction between soul and spirit. The soul comprises our thoughts, mind, and emotions. The spirit is our flame, so to speak—the part of us that connects us to the Lord. And the living Word of God brings a distinction between soul and spirit, judging the attitudes of our hearts—which in turn determine our actions. When the Word of God is the focus of our soul, our spirit will respond in faith and power, and actions motivated by faith will follow. But when we focus on negative words and circumstances, we respond with fleshly emotions like doubt, anger, hurt, and fear. Guess what follows? Actions. We run, hide, lash out, or quit. Weariness and burnout happens when we focus too long on the wrong voice or the wrong words.

Before Jezebel came along to burst his bubble, Elijah acted in faith and power because he had been listening to and believing in the voice of the Holy Spirit and the Word of almighty God. There is a reason he was called a prophet. Elijah listened to God's Word and believed it and acted upon it.

This man of God didn't become weary in his well-doing because of Jezebel's words; the weariness came upon him when he moved out of the spirit and into his flesh. He began to listen to, believe in, and act upon the voice of this woman and her words. Her words and threats sent him into a tailspin because they directed his eyes inward instead of upward. Fear and discouragement took over because he was looking at himself and his weaknesses. This prophet of God thought he was all alone because he permitted her words against him to replace God's living and active words. Satan, of course, knows how quickly personal attacks have a way of knocking the wind out of our sails.

## An African Story

I, for one, recognize Elijah's fear because I've felt it myself. At the risk of being a little vulnerable, let me pull back the curtain on my own tailspin experience. It was on my very first mission trip to Uganda. My African friend, Monique, had been pleading with me for three years to come to her country and hold a women's conference. I did a lot of speaking around the United States, but Africa was a whole other ballgame. It took the Holy Spirit practically shoving me onto the plane to get me to go, but when the time came, I *knew* he was sending me.

But even more than traveling alone across the globe to an African nation, adjusting to pit latrines, and sleeping under mosquito nets, I was apprehensive over how to speak to people in this foreign culture, and a developing-world culture at that. How would my U.S. Christianity translate? These weren't American women. These were smiling Ugandan ladies in colorful dresses with babies tied to their backs. Many traveled from distances on foot, and they were hungry and eager to hear the wisdom that would flow from the *muzungu's* (white woman's) mouth.

I knew God brought me to Uganda for a purpose, but the more I observed the cultural differences, the more unsure of myself I became. In the months before my trip, I prayed over the messages, poring over the Word of God and listening for the Holy Spirit's direction. I spent a lot of time praying for the women, asking God to prepare their hearts and to have his way. I surrendered myself to the Holy Spirit's leading, and when the day came, I was prepared—body, soul, and spirit, confident that God had guided me in my preparations.

Praying nonstop the first few days as I got to know Monique and John Mubiru, their children, their friends, and their home, my fears slowly gave way to a peace I couldn't explain. In my spirit, I knew the gospel was clearly presented in my messages, and I just had to trust God with what he gave me to bring to the women of Uganda. Even though I felt peace about the words that God gave me to preach, I was still nervous, because my messages contained a lot of personal stories to illustrate my points. Worried, I kept questioning how these precious Ugandan women would relate to me and my American life. When the conference began, I was somehow able to set my jitters aside and take that step of faith like Elijah, acting upon the words God had given me.

On the first day, I shared my own personal testimony, telling of God's faithfulness to me as a single mom, raising three children without help, and struggling to buy food and pay my rent. I couldn't tell by looking at the women's faces if they had any idea what I was talking about. My story painted a simple picture of how God can create something beautiful out of a hurting and broken life when we finally surrender it to him.

## In the Cave

The day ended well, but then my eyes drifted inward and doubt crept into my thoughts. Lying under my mosquito net, I broke down and cried. I was disappointed with myself for being so foolish as to travel all the way to Uganda just to talk about myself and my American problems, when these people lack many of the basic necessities that I have so readily available and often take for granted. This was just the first day of a weeklong women's conference, which was to be followed by another weeklong conference in Kenya. And after that, we'd return to Uganda and speak in several villages in the bush. Overwhelmed, I fell asleep under the mosquito net, covering myself with a blanket woven from my own shortcomings and insecurities.

We all have our tailspin experiences, and they usually happen when we, like Elijah, transition from the spirit to our flesh, diverting our eyes away from God and his Word onto ourselves, other people, or other circumstances. Even in our greatest moments of victory, one negative word spoken in the midst of thousands of voices of praise can cause us to look inward and question, "Who do you think you are?" And all of a sudden, we're ready to throw in the towel and run for a cave in the hills.

If we take up permanent residence in this spiritual cave, weariness will overtake us, our flame will burn out, and we'll never complete the work God has for us—nor will we experience the joy and satisfaction that serving the Lord can bring.

Well, we can't leave the old prophet in his cave. If we go back to Elijah's story, we'll find him feeling sorry for himself, fearing for his life, and wanting to die. He couldn't have lifted himself up by his sandal straps even if he had wanted to. Yet even though the prophet's eyes were diverted onto himself, God never left him, nor had he given up on him. There was still work for Elijah to do.

God didn't abandon him or even condemn him. There were no harsh words of judgment. God knew where he was and how he got there, and loved him anyway. He wasn't finished with Elijah, but he also understood Elijah's humanity, and provided a bread cake and jar of water as refreshment. God even sent an angel to encourage him to partake of this nourishment.

That's the good news about becoming weary in our well-doing. God appreciates what we do for him, even if no one else does. He sees when we become frustrated, hurt, depressed, angry, or defeated, and he sends the refreshment we need to strengthen our depleted spirits for the next leg of our journey.

Just try and wrap your mind around this: almighty God, creator of the universe, King of all kings, loves and cares about us enough to actually *serve* us. It's never God giving up on us—we give up on ourselves because we listen to, believe in, and act upon the wrong words. But God, in his mercy, is still talking to us. We just need to get up and eat.

## Get Up and Eat!

The angel encouraged Elijah to get up and eat so he would be strong enough to continue, saying: "Arise, eat, because the journey is too great for you" (1 Kings 19:7 NASB). God knew what Elijah would need for his journey; he provided it, prepared it, and prodded him to partake of it.

When Elijah was ready, he showed him how to once again tune in to the true Word of God. To truly hear what God was saying, Elijah had to shut out all the other voices in his head, along with his preconceived ideas about how God would speak to him and lead him in his service. God didn't reveal himself in strong winds, earthquakes, or fire. He revealed himself in a still, quiet voice.

That is exactly what God does for us too. He knows all the twists, turns, hills, and valleys of the journey he wants to take us on. He knows what will sustain us on the journey, no matter what work he has called us to. He also provides what we need when we need it, because he is on our side and by our side.

In case you might be wondering how my first Ugandan experience ended, let's just say God can reach even a slow learner like me. The next day, I prepared new messages that were birthed out of my fears, and (big surprise) I fell flat on my face. Returning to the

Mubirus' home, I felt completely defeated. Like Elijah, I retreated to my own little cave of self-pity.

But God knew where I was hiding, and like he did for Elijah, he sent an angel to refresh me and get me back on track. We were all gathered together for the evening meal when a knock at the door called Monique out of the room. After a few minutes, she came back and signaled for me to come. I excused myself from the rest of the family and followed her outside. There on the porch was a tearful woman whom Monique introduced as Florence.

## Florence

Florence didn't speak English, so speaking in Luganda, she told Monique what was troubling her. She wanted me to pray for her and give her counsel, and she shared how she felt moved by my story the day before. Florence felt the same feelings of anger, hurt, and bitterness growing in her heart toward her husband that I expressed in my testimony. She was devastated, because she just discovered she was pregnant and that her husband was taking a second wife.

Of course, in the United States, I had never counseled anyone whose husband was in a polygamous relationship, much less moving the new wife into the home. But the Holy Spirit directed me to take my eyes off of these cultural differences and myself and concentrate on this woman's hurting heart. We talked for some time, and then we prayed. Before Florence left, she hugged me and shed new tears of peace, which could only have come from God.

I was completely amazed that this woman came to me, an American woman. I asked Monique about it, and she said it was because the Holy Spirit used my testimony to touch her. She actually connected with me and saw herself in my story—my American story!

Like he did for Elijah, God provided nourishment for my weary spirit. After I sat up and started eating what God prepared for me, my spirit regained strength, and the focus of my eyes was once again on the Lord, instead of myself. God had to nudge me along to take the nourishment he was giving me for my African journey, and to trust him again so I could throw away the messages I'd prepared out of fear.

I didn't have to understand how my messages would fit into the African culture; I just needed to trust that God gave them to me, and that he wanted me to deliver them to those women out of obedience. How they were received and any spiritual work to be done in their hearts was God's responsibility, not mine.

For the rest of that week, one by one, women came to me—some to the house, some after the services, some by way of sent notes. Each bore a similar declaration and request for prayer: *your story is my story; God is telling me to forgive, to love, to receive his love—will you pray for me?* This was a sweet confirmation that the Holy Spirit was using the lessons he taught me in the United States to touch the lives of women in Uganda, on the other side of the world. Wow!

Several months after returning to the United States from that first mission trip, Monique contacted me to tell me that Florence gave birth to a beautiful daughter, whom she named after me. Little Terri, as she is known in Uganda, is a living, breathing testimony and reminder to me of how God can use anyone, in any way he chooses, if they will just keep their eyes focused on Jesus and his Word.

# Chapter 12

# Walking Wounded

"There are times when we cannot cry at all, and then he cries in us."

—Charles Spurgeon

**Before we can move forward** in fanning the flame that once blazed in our spirit, we have to cut away the charred wick that's left us smoldering. Nothing can douse a flaming spirit faster than wounds inflicted on us by people within the church. We are all supposed to be on the same side, fighting a common enemy, the devil, and promoting the same agenda of furthering the kingdom of God by saving the lost and discipling new believers in the truth of the gospel. But sadly, multitudes of God's warriors carry wounds and scars deep within their souls. These are the walking wounded, people hurt by church people. Like bruised reeds and smoldering wicks, the walking wounded struggle to hang on to their faith.

In this part of our pilgrimage, we will be taking a few steps inward to uncover one of the most subtle and damaging schemes of the enemy to cripple and disable the body of Christ, the church.

These are the betrayals, broken confidences, attacks, and wounds that come from within the church. Once exposed, we will cut away the charred places and pour on the soothing balm to bring restoration and healing to wounds that have festered for far too long.

## Help Yourself First

As many flights as I have taken in my travels, I can almost recite the flight attendants' safety speech in my sleep:

> Ladies and gentlemen, please take out the safety cards found in the seat pocket in front of you. . . . In the unlikely event of an emergency and loss of cabin pressure, an oxygen mask will fall in front of you from an overhead compartment. . . . If you are traveling with children or are seated next to someone who needs assistance, please place the mask on yourself first, and then offer assistance . . .

No matter what nation or airline, and in every language, the message is always the same—take care of yourself first. This kind of goes against the grain of Christian thought, which tells us to prefer others before ourselves and that if we want to be first, we should be last. And in normal circumstances, we should put others first. But the reasoning behind taking care of yourself first when cabin pressure is lost is so that you will have all the oxygen you need to fully function so you can help someone who can't help themselves. The same rule applies to us in the body of Christ when there is a loss of spiritual oxygen. We can't help anyone else spiritually if we are hurt or incapacitated.

Whenever we've been hurt or wounded by people, particularly in the church, it is important that we take care of ourselves and treat the wound. We need to be spiritually whole and healthy before we can offer help to anyone else.

## Enemy within the Camp

During the Vietnam War, my dad was a major in the Army and a military advisor who helped formulate plans against the enemy. Because of his rank and his position as commanding officer, he was a target. On one occasion, as he and his men were riding back to camp in his jeep, they encountered the enemy on the road. Gunfire and a battle ensued, and my dad and his men were able to take them down. After searching the fallen Vietcong soldiers, my dad discovered a map in one of their shirt pockets. The map was a detailed drawing of the U.S. compound, highlighting my father's quarters with a big red X on his bed.

My dad told me they frequently moved their sleeping quarters around, just in case there might be informants in the camp; but this map was up-to-date and his bed was clearly marked. I thank God the enemy's scheme was discovered before they could carry out their plans against my father. But the truth of the matter is that the enemy came from within my father's own camp. Only allies who were the most trusted and closest to my dad could have known which barracks were his and where he slept.

If you are a Christ follower, you're automatically a target with a big red X on your back. Unsettling as this may be, we have to recognize that Satan will use whatever means he has at his disposal to destroy us, even using trusted people from within the church. Perhaps the most troubling and heart-wrenching aspect of this particular tactic, making these wounds the most difficult to overcome, is the fact that these attacks come from within our own camp.

Scripture passages often portray us as being in spiritual warfare, and they provide instructions for putting on the full armor of God and taking up our weapons. Scripture talks about knowing the schemes of the enemy and being obedient to carry out the will of God. We are in God's army. We get that.

We are prepared and expect to do battle with the enemy, knowing there are a lot of weapons formed against us in the world. But the most difficult and wearying battles are the ones fought against church members who have formed weapons against us.

Before I go any further, let me first say this: People are not our enemy. Satan is the enemy. Satan uses people to carry out his tactics, and he's not picky about whether they go to church or not. We know he is the accuser of the brethren (Rev. 12:10). We know Satan is the father of lies, and we know that he is out to steal, kill, and destroy. But we also know in whom we believe, the life giver, and we have experienced his gift of an abundant life.

The war we are fighting is spiritual. Like Paul told the Ephesian church, "For our struggle is not against flesh and blood, but against the rulers, against the authorities, against the powers of this dark world and against the spiritual forces of evil in the heavenly realms" (Eph. 6:12 NIV).

## The Church, a Living Organism

The church is the body of Christ. It has been described as an organism, something that is alive. It is not a building or an organization where there are only programs and protocol. The organism called the church is described in the book of Acts. If we stay in the Word and operate according to it, the church will grow and produce good cells and multiply and multiply and multiply. It will become the family that God intended, with all its parts working together as in a body. The body of Christ is made up of millions of cells, functioning much like a human body. And just like the human body, when cancer is introduced, it will kill some or all of a body if left untreated.

I once talked with a retired pastor and friend about this cancer in the church. Here's what my friend, pastor Dale, said: "As we read the New Testament, we see how to extract cancer out of the body of Christ. When hateful people are in the church and they just want to hurt and cause division, they have to be dealt with according to the Scriptures and with love." He explained:

> These are very hard things to do—to sit down with someone and confront them with their sin and hurtful attitude and then show them how it is hurting others as well as the church. Their pride usually will not allow them to come under the authority of the church for their restoration and even salvation. They will either accuse the leadership of hurting them or of wrongdoing, or they'll make accusations about something they hope will hurt the leadership.

Pastor Dale concluded by saying,

> All of these things take their toll on the leadership of the church, but those kinds of hurts and accusations stay with you a long time.
>
> Pastors and leaders are called to shepherd the church. When wolves get in, we have to guard to flock. The wolf might bite and scar us, but in the end, we still have the flock God gave us to shepherd. And we should know that we have done the master's work by keeping

them safe. We find our satisfaction and accomplishment in Jesus for the work he has given us to do.

## Christ Followers and Church Members

This organism, the church, is full of growing cells, and it is often infected with the cancer of the world, which causes great sickness. Sick people, sin-sick people, make up the church. Some acknowledge the lordship of Christ in their lives and are on a journey to become his disciples. But some people accept the church (their congregation or denomination) as their lord. They continue their journey of attendance and sometimes even dedicated service to their lord, the church. These people believe their church is an organization in which if they do this and that and follow this program or that protocol, everything will run smoothly and everyone in the church will be happy. They believe that when a man or woman in the church does what he or she should be doing, he or she will grow in Christ. But if you've been around church for very long, you know this just isn't the case.

When talking about the church, we have to segregate people into two groups: born-again followers of Christ and church members. Church members don't understand spiritual things, but they do understand programs and protocol. "We've never done it like that before" is often their battle cry. They work to take things back to where they are comfortable, even if it means running the pastor off, or at least tearing him down to "put him back in his place."

Clashes between Christ followers and church members are often where wounds occur. You probably have a few scars and stories of your own, but here are two familiar scenarios:

A Christ follower teaching Sunday school digs a little deeper into the Scripture, encouraging discussion on becoming more like Jesus, but is reprimanded for not sticking to the program. Frustrated and hurt, he leaves the church.

A longtime Christ-following woman desires to start a ministry to bring the older and younger women together in her church after being greatly blessed and seeing a lot of growth in a young lady she has been mentoring. But shortly after launching her mentoring program, a church member who believes they know better about how to do this begins to micromanage and second-guess every decision. The lady gives up and quits. Both she and the women she started working with are hurt.

Pastors probably have the most difficult job: managing staff, keeping their eyes on the finances, preparing to minister to the congregation, counseling the hurting, and so on. Keeping their heart in the ministry is hard. They often want to pull back and not put in so much love because it makes them vulnerable to the next church member, or even their own staff members, who decide they can do the job much better, even though many people have no idea what a pastor's life is like or what he does all day.

Whenever a follower of Christ is attacked or wounded by someone from within the church, it's personal and it hurts, probably even worse than an attack from someone outside the church. When we suffer from a wound inflicted by "one of our own," we feel betrayed.

## Betrayal

Betrayal from within the church is probably one of the hardest wounds to overcome. After talking to pastor Dale about the walking wounded in the body of Christ, I asked if he had personally ever experienced this kind of betrayal. He had, and he gave me permission to share his story:

Several years ago, four friends and myself got together. The five of us wanted to establish a New Testament type, Elder-led church, as opposed to the traditional, majority-led church we were all accustomed to. We met several times to establish what that would mean and how the church leadership would be in partnership with the Executive and Senior Pastors of the church to help accomplish the vision the Pastors believed was coming from God.

Because we were all friends and had served together in our church for quite some time, everyone felt confident that together, our vision could be realized. In fact, two of the Elders and I were very close friends. Everyone called us the Three Amigos. I felt they would help stay the course and protect me and the other pastor if dissensions would arise. The first year went great. The church was growing and we had the freedom to lead. Ministry and missions were established along with goals to accomplish them.

After the first year, the existing chairman of Elders rolled off and another chairman was selected from among the Elders. I had known the newly elected chairman since he was a college student. I attended his wedding, went on retreats with him, and our families often had dinner together. We were very close. But when he took over the chairman's role, he decided he was over the church, and the pastors should be following him. I was the Executive Pastor, and he brought me a list of rules that our staff should be following and what we needed to ask him permission for.

Because the Chairman's demands completely contradicted what had previously been established for our church model, I brought it up in the meeting with the Elders. The chairman exploded and told me that I might not respect him, but I surely would respect the office of chairman. I told him it wasn't about respect because he was undermining the Elder-led, New Testament type of church we had just established. Instead of having my back and standing up for me and all the work we had put into the establishment of our church model over the last year, my two best buddies didn't want to say anything for fear of making someone angry. I felt betrayed, but we all agreed to pray about it and try to understand what was happening. I left the meeting trying to decide my fate. I didn't want to be in a place where someone who comes to church three hours a week dictates what the church does and where it goes.

What happened next caught me completely off guard. After the meeting, the chairman followed me out to my car, and starting yelling at me and hurling accusations. I tried to stay calm because things were escalating pretty quickly, and I asked him what had gotten into him and why he was doing this. After more yelling, he got right in my face and told me not to come back the next day. I told him the church installed me as pastor and the church, not him, would have to dismiss me. I came home pretty beat down and wounded. I had no idea why my friend turned on me the way he did.

As soon as he got home, the chairman called all the other elders, giving a skewed account of our parking lot confrontation. It broke my heart that anyone would think that I would treat anyone like he said I did.

To make a long story short, I stayed on as Executive Pastor and the Chairman remained as well. But our Elders meetings never were the same after that. The whole complexion of our leadership team was changed.

I realize now it was a power play. He just wanted to be in charge so he could be recognized for orchestrating our church's growth and progress. After about ten years and many attempts on my part for reconciliation, he called me and asked if I would come to his office. I agreed.

When I walked in, he came to the door, extending his hand to greet me. He then apologized for all the stuff he had done to me and said about me. I was proud of him for putting his pride aside and apologizing.

As a side note, I saw him recently. We hugged like old school mates and just gushed all over each other. It was good to see him and I felt like he reciprocated my affection. Only God can bring healing and complete reconciliation as he did for the chairman and myself.

I appreciate pastor Dale sharing his story, because it confirms to all of us that there is hope for the afflicted—even those betrayed and wounded in the church.

## Affliction's Hope

Think of Christ on the night of the Last Supper. While everyone was gathered around the table, he looked at Judas and said, "Go do what you must do" (paraphrased). And then Jesus went on to do what his Father commissioned him to do, which included dying on the cross.

There are Judases who will betray us, but we have been commissioned by Father God to fulfill our call in the ministry, whatever that ministry might be. We can't allow our flame to die out because of opposition or betrayal.

We are to walk in the footsteps of the Savior and strive to love, forgive, and continue to reflect Christ to a lost and dying world. We can only do that if we keep Christ at the forefront of our lives. As soon as we start looking at our circumstances and our situations with our human eyes, we will start to sink, just like Peter. But once we realize the answer is standing there in the water with us and we cry out, "Help me, Jesus! I'm sinking!" he will immediately reach out his hand, lift us up, and walk with us back to safe haven.

In his book *Desiring God*, John Piper looks at a passage from Romans and makes a very good point about the hope we gain from our afflictions:

> Paul says, "We rejoice in our sufferings, knowing that suffering produces endurance, and endurance produces character, and character produces hope" (Rom. 5:3–4 ESV).
>
> Here, Paul's joy is not merely rooted in his great reward, but in the effect of suffering to solidify his hope in that reward. Afflictions produce endurance, and endurance produces a sense that our faith is real and genuine, and that strengthens our hope that we will indeed gain Christ.[1]

Our faith is real and genuine, even if our smoldering wick feels like it's going out. We can fan it back into a blazing fire again if we choose to surrender our affliction to God, forgive the perpetrator, and take hold of the hope we have in Christ.

The strength and character we gain from our hurtful experiences will not only be greater than our losses, but because we've had that battle experience, we become even wiser adversaries against our enemy's future schemes. That's exactly what Satan fears the most—a follower of Christ who understands Satan's demonic schemes and takes a stand to resist him. He will flee because he can see we are fully armed, taking up powerful weapons to wage war against him in the name of our king.

## Note

[1]John Piper, *Desiring God,* revised edition (Colorado Springs, CO: Multnomah Books, 2011), 283–84.

# Chapter 13

# Watching the Weary

"If our words are not consistent with our actions,
they will never be heard above the thunder of our deeds."

—H. Burke Peterson

The next step in our pilgrimage has to do with all the people we may have touched on our Christian journey and how the light of our spiritual lamp affects them. Even though we may struggle to walk the talk of our faith, there are always those who are watching and even imitating us.

## Mini-Mes

Just living life, we don't even think about all the eyes on us, especially in our families. Much of what we do around our children and grandchildren is caught, not taught. As soon as they're born, we start working on turning them into little mini-mes—some even start before birth. I have a friend whose daughter will be having her first baby (a boy) in a few months. The father is a huge fan of the Ole Miss college football team, so it was no big surprise that they decorated the baby's room in red and blue. I guarantee that child will grow up loving Ole Miss, just like his dad.

There's nothing new about children copying their parents. When my son was born, my three-year-old daughter mimicked everything I did as a mommy. She changed her own baby's diapers, sang songs, rocked him to sleep, and fed him—exactly how she saw me do those things for her baby brother.

Parents not only instill their likes and passions into their children, they also instill their values and beliefs. If the parents are committed Christians who read their Bibles every day and pray over meals, the child will often catch that and do the same. And if the parents have bad habits, children will typically imitate and pick them up.

When I was a little girl (I know this is going to date me), most adults smoked cigarettes. This was before it was a public taboo. Parents could buy their children packs of candy cigarettes. My mom was a smoker, and I loved getting one of the white candy cigarette sticks with the red-lit end from my own pack and pretend to smoke like Mommy. I watched when Mom knocked off the ashes, and I bit my candy down to the same length to be just like her. Bad as that may sound, it is what often happens in life—children imitate their parents.

Mini-mes also exist in other settings. I had a high school English teacher who encouraged me to write, a dad who taught me work ethic, and a pastor who instilled the importance of memorizing Scripture. Each of them impacted my life in different ways, and they probably have no idea how much influence they had on me. I can't remember the name of my English teacher, but you wouldn't be reading this book right now if it hadn't been for her encouraging words all those years ago.

The apostle Paul understood the value of mentorship and discipleship, and went so far as to *encourage* people to imitate him, just as he imitated Christ (1 Cor. 11:1). Talk about risky! Can you imagine asking people, "Do as I do, respond I like I respond, live your life like I live mine"?

But the truth is, we really don't have to ask anyone because, just like our children, they're already watching, imitating, and following in our steps. Very little we do or say doesn't have some kind of effect on the people in our lives—the words we say and the actions we take influence others for the good as well as for the bad. Christians are always on call.

God sees, knows, and understands your life, including your challenges and your weariness, and he doesn't want you to give up. You are a lamp in the darkness, and if your flame should go out, what would happen to those who look to that light? God not only wants to strengthen you, but he also wants to revive and reignite you in your faith—for your sake, and also for those whose lives you affect.

## A Weary King

King David, near the end of his reign over Israel, had yet another battle to fight with his old enemy, the Philistines: "Once again the Philistines were at war with Israel. And when David and his men were in the thick of battle, David became weak and exhausted" (2 Sam. 21:15 NLT).

David might have been killed if it weren't for a brave soldier named Abishai who came along at just the right moment to save his life from the Philistine who had his sights set on David. What happens next is what I want to zoom in on. Verse 17 tells us that when David's men saw how close their king came to death because of his weariness, they made a group decision: "You are not going out to battle with us again! Why risk snuffing out the light of Israel?" (2 Sam. 21:17 NLT). These men recognized how valuable the light of their beloved king's lamp was to the nation of Israel.

In David's case, the weariness and exhaustion were physical because of his age, but the same principle can be applied to those of us who have been out in the trenches fighting spiritual battles for years. Like King David, we do what we know we need to do—go out to battle and fight the good fight of faith. But we get tired in the fight. When we become weary spiritually, we aren't as sharp as we once were, and that makes us vulnerable to the enemy's attack.

For me, as a ministry leader, I can become overly involved in all the needs of my mission in Uganda, which includes putting together a short-term mission team, fundraising, preparing messages for speaking, writing articles, newsletters, counseling, and answering emails—and all that on top of the pressures of being a mom to a huge family. Every Sunday after church, everyone gathers for Sunday dinner at my house. There can be anywhere from eight to twenty-five people around the table. With such a big family, it isn't uncommon that a birthday or anniversary is also celebrated, and that, of course, adds to the preparation. I'm not complaining. I love my ministry and my family, but I do become weary.

## This Little Light of Mine

There was a time when my own lamp was barely flickering. Though I was going to church and managing my ministry, I was as close to burnout as I have ever been. As I said before, I did a lot of work in Uganda, partnering with my Ugandan friends. There were several people to manage the work over there, but here in the United

States, it was just me. I didn't have a staff of people to help, and I still had all of my family to take care of.

My work in Uganda included a children's school sponsorship program which had about three hundred children registered at that time. That meant I had to keep up with the sponsors in the United States and collect the sponsor payments and wire funds to Uganda for tuition. I was also always trying to find new sponsors for children on the waiting list. At the same time, we were building a hospital. The plan was for a three-story building. The first two floors were built and functioning, but there remained a third floor to be constructed. I managed the funds to keep the hospital running, and in addition, I had been trying to raise money for completion of the construction. Plus, I organized and led short-term mission teams to Uganda—we conducted pastors' conferences, women's conferences, children's crusades, medical missions, etc.

After my book on blended families was released, I was contracted to write a monthly column for a LifeWay publication. This led to a lot of speaking and traveling in the United States. My ministry was growing, and God opened a lot of other doors for ministry to women, as well as other mission opportunities.

During my season of spiritual burnout, there were times when I felt like quitting everything. To be truthful, I still have occasional moments like that. But a lot of people depended on me, particularly the children in our sponsorship program. At home, I continued on as usual, but grew increasingly dissatisfied with church. To be clear, the problem wasn't with the church—it was with me. I started pulling back from activities and from Sunday evening and mid-week services. I just wanted to stay home and do nothing. I didn't want to be responsible for anyone other than myself.

I studied the Bible to prepare messages and prayed for God to bless the work I was doing, but the passion and pursuit to go deeper were gone. My relationship with Jesus was suffering under all the busyness of the work I was doing for him.

I hadn't walked away from God, and I hadn't stopped believing and trusting in him. I was just tired and weary. Every time I got an email from Uganda telling me they needed money for this or for that, I sank deeper into a funk. When the deadline for my monthly article drew near, I just didn't feel like writing it. Ministry work can feel like a black hole at times. It never fills up, no matter how much heart, time, energy, and money you put into it.

## Spiritual Sickness

Recently I got sick and ran a high temperature of over 103 degrees over several days. When I finally went to see a doctor, they immediately admitted me to the hospital. My white blood cell count was 28,000 (normal is around 9,000). A bacterial infection was raging in my body. If I had continued to ignore it by just treating the surface symptoms with fever reducers, it would have continued to escalate and I might have gone into septic shock. That can kill you.

Much like a high fever is an indication that something is wrong with your physical body, the lack of passion for church, Scriptures, and time in prayer are indicators of spiritual weariness. If we keep on going and ignore the warning signs, we will not only become more weak and vulnerable, but we will run the risk of spiritual burnout.

Spiritual sickness alone can weaken us, but we also have an enemy, Satan, who will take full advantage of our vulnerability. We are ripe for the enemy to swoop in with temptations that play to our weaknesses, and that is where many fall into sin and moral failures. Just like the Philistine set his sights on taking down King David, the devil will use every tactic in the book to destroy us. He will hit us hard where it hurts the most, and when we stumble or trip up, he'll kick us when we're down.

We aren't doing anyone any favors to keep on going without addressing our spiritual health. We need to go to the doctor, to the great physician who heals not just our body, but also our soul and spirit. Great men and women of God have fallen into sin by ignoring the warning signs. When they fell, many who depended on the light cast from their lamps fell with them. I'm in no way saying people worshipped them, but they did see them as leaders in the faith, showing them the way. They are like the people in the churches Paul wrote to in his Epistles who trusted him to show them how to live and walk out their faith in Jesus Christ. How we live out our Christianity affects the people around us, whether we like it or not.

The good news is that we serve an all-knowing, all-loving God who knows our strengths and our weaknesses. Nothing is hidden from his sight, and he is always right there to help. He is our healer. Jesus didn't just save us to send us out to conquer the world. Yes, he does give us work to do for the kingdom and he did ask us to be lights in the darkness, but he is the ultimate light of the world, and he said he would never leave us or forsake us. We are Jesus's hands and feet on earth to go and carry out the charge he gives us—but building the kingdom is ultimately the work of God, not us.

## Stepping Back

If we take the example of a vulnerable King David a step further, his men knew the only way to preserve the lamp of Israel was to remove him from the fight. Now, I'm not saying we can just remove ourselves from the battles of life and from everything we are doing. But I am saying there are times, when our spiritual health is in the balance, that we need to step back to take a hard, honest look at everything we are involved in, and then ask the Holy Spirit to show us if there is something he wants us to take off our plate, even if it is only for a season while we strengthen ourselves in the Lord.

During the time of my own spiritual weariness, I knew I couldn't keep on going at the pace I had been accustomed to. It was in December, at the end of a long year, that I decided to lay it all out before the Lord. I knew people depended on me, but I also knew I wouldn't be doing anyone any good if I lost *my* way. I removed myself from the battle, and got alone with the Lord to fast and pray.

When I say I laid it all out before the Lord, that's exactly what I did. I listed everything I was involved in in ministry, including writing, speaking, missions, and family—I left out nothing. Just going over the list overwhelmed me, so I got completely honest with Jesus.

I was halfway hoping God would say something like, "Well done, good and faithful servant, enter into the joy of the Lord," so I could just wipe my hands and walk away. But I knew that wouldn't happen, so I asked for help instead, literally. If God wanted me to continue doing the work, especially all the work in Uganda with the sponsorship program, then I really needed someone to come alongside and help me, someone who would care about the children like I did. And God knew how little I could afford to pay this person who would have to have a heart for the Lord and this work. In addition to my plea for help, I also told the Lord I was willing to let go of other parts of the ministry, if that was his will. I just wanted to be spiritually well again.

Nothing changed overnight, but this became my daily prayer. Over the next few months, several things happened. My cousin, a corporate trainer, came to visit me and helped me lay out a strategic plan for my ministry. While she was here and while we were breaking the ministry down into seven categories, God began to nudge me and show me that there were some areas of the ministry that I could let go of, at least temporarily. There was nothing wrong with them, but in this season, God was asking me to take them off my plate so I would have more time with him and more time to be able to minister more effectively in other areas. It was hard, but I immediately began to turn down those ministry opportunities. Even though I was a bit disappointed and saddened by it, I felt a tremendous weight lifted.

Then God began to raise up helpers. A few good friends who know me well and have been close to my ministry volunteered to come in and do bookwork, stuff envelopes, print and send out receipts for donations, and more. Another weight was lifted.

One of the ladies who volunteered regularly, Tracy, was a nurse in my church. I consulted with her often on medical questions that came up for our hospital in Uganda. She ended up going to Uganda on a medical mission, and the Holy Spirit hooked her with a love for the nation and the African people—she even returned to the United States with a newly sponsored child. Tracy helped me to gather and categorize all the medical supplies and equipment for a container I was preparing to ship. I grew to depend on her for much of the Ugandan work, and because she had been there, she understood what it was all about.

Before I realized it, I had the help I had prayed for, and God even worked out the finances so she could continue to be a part of the ministry on a more permanent basis. Today, Tracy is my administrative assistant and the managing director of our Child Sponsorship Program. Other than the executive decisions she brings to me, Tracy manages and oversees everything on both the U.S. and Ugandan sides. She even spends a month in Uganda every other year to get current information and pictures of all the children, both sponsored and unsponsored. Only God could have done this.

I'm sharing this story because God does tell us in his Word that he will not give us more than we can handle. And he does give us a way of escape so we can hold up through temptation, testing, or time of trial (1 Cor. 10:13). But we do need to go to him when we are running that spiritual fever, which is an indication of a problem that only he can heal. He not only heals, but he answers prayer, even for things that seem impossible to us. I never could figure out the answer to my weariness, and because of the amazing way God worked everything out, he gets all the praise and glory.

If I had ignored the symptoms of weariness in my life, allowing my lamp to go out, a lot of people might have been affected— my family and friends, as well as those whose lives my ministry touches in the United States and around the world. But even if you don't have a "ministry" per se, as a believer, your spiritual health matters. People are watching you, depending on you, and trusting you as a light in the darkness. The enemy is just hoping to get a foot in the door of your heart to bring you down, along with all of those watching you.

Even if you're not a pastor, teacher, ministry leader, or another type of church leader, you still have influence in the world, and you are a light reflecting faith in God, regardless of how dimly or brightly your own lamp might be burning. I know I'm not the only one out there who has been in this place. And believe me, ministry workers aren't the only ones who burn out. Moms with babies tugging at them all day and dads who never seem to find time off work are also among this number. Spiritual sickness can happen when bills are piling up or when physical health deteriorates. Unforeseen tragedy or loss can also knock the spiritual wind from our sails.

Unfortunately, even though we might be struggling to keep our head above water, the eyes watching us don't just look the other way. They're still watching, sometimes even more intently, to see how our profession of faith holds true under adverse circumstances.

God knows what we need before we even ask him, but we do have to ask. He is waiting for us to take a step back, to lay it all before him, and to ask him to do whatever it will take to meet us in our need and bring us back to spiritual health.

We just need to pay attention to the symptoms and take action by going to the Lord. After finally doing this myself, I was completely amazed at how he answered every prayer, lightened my burden, and revived me spiritually. God doesn't show favoritism (Rom. 2:11), nor does he lie. God always follows through with what he says he will do (Num. 23:19). If God would do the impossible for me, he will do it for you.

# Chapter 14

# A Servant's Reward

"One of the principle rules of religion is
to lose no occasion to serving God.
And since He is invisible to our eyes, we are
to serve Him in our neighbor . . ."

—John Wesley

**When I was a kid,** Mom occasionally left my brother to babysit my younger brothers and me. George, of course, saw this as a prime opportunity to get us siblings to do all his unwanted chores. With the snap of a dishtowel to our backsides, we became his servants. Servanthood to my brother was short-lived, though; it only lasted until we figured out there were more dishtowels in the drawer and we could snap back.

The definition of "servant" is "one that serves others,"[1] like cleaning George's room and taking out the trash for him. You may not have had a dictator for a big brother, but for many of us, the idea of being a servant is a negative concept. Scripturally, the word "slave" is often used interchangeably with "servant." Slavery brings up images of people who are used and abused, forced to do their master's will against their own. The idea of taking on the role of a slave or servant for the rest of my life doesn't sound very appealing to me.

If you've ever felt offended or unappreciated while serving others, servanthood may have even left a bad taste in your mouth. The very nature of servitude is to make yourself subject to the one you're serving. That takes a lot of humility, and goes against our human nature.

Why would Jesus call us to be servants to others? There has to be more to it than the definition states. When we are in a spiritually low place, it can be hard to find motivation to do the things we were once passionate about, and potentially even more difficult if that means serving others. But he is there to help us push through to do what we don't feel like doing. Like so many other biblical principles, when we apply them to our lives, we get back the opposite of what we would expect, and so much more.

Jesus often contradicted traditional thought on how to live out the law of God. He taught his disciples to love people by going the second mile—when someone asks for your shirt, give him your jacket as well. Jesus told those striving for recognition and position that if they wanted to be great, they should take the least position. If they wanted to be first, be last.

Throughout Scripture, we find examples of how God would have us treat people with love: "A soft answer turns away wrath" (Prov. 15:1 ESV), "pray for them that despitefully use you" (Luke 6:28 ASV), and more. So it's no surprise that Jesus would call us to be servants to others in love.

## Elisha

Serving in love is an important concept, one that can be hard to wrap our heads around. But just as there is unexpected reward for obedience to do things that go against our human grain, there is also unexpected reward for serving when that service is done with the right heart. Scripture tells us that if we want to receive, we first need to give. That's where being a servant comes in. Serving is giving in love.

In Scripture, many men and women answered the call to servanthood, but I'd like to zoom in on one in particular: Elisha. He first comes on the scene in 1 Kings 19. God instructed Elijah to go find Elisha, and anoint him to be his successor as prophet in the land.

Elijah found Elisha plowing behind twelve teams of oxen. Elijah went up to Elisha while he was working in the field and threw his mantle on him. Just the fact that there were twelve teams of oxen is a pretty good indication that Elisha came from a family of substance. The young prophet understood what this gesture by Elijah meant. In essence, Elijah was saying, "Follow me. I am passing the mantle of my prophetic office on to you."

Elisha didn't hesitate to leave everything. In fact, he slaughtered the oxen pulling his plow, burned the wood from the plow to cook them, and served up the meat to family and friends. He kissed his parents goodbye and followed Elijah. Scripture says he became Elijah's servant. That's it. It doesn't make sense. Elisha was a young man from a wealthy family, and he gave it all up to become a servant. Why? Because Elisha stood to gain far more in his servitude than he would give up in family wealth. His gain was spiritual—sitting at the feet and learning from the master on how to hear, discern, and speak the Word of God. He was ever watching and observing not only how Elijah dealt with people as a prophet, but witnessing the power of God in the amazing miracles he performed at Elijah's hand and word.

After the old prophet threw the mantle on Elisha, nothing more is said of him until at least four years had passed—some commentaries say up to twelve years. But Elisha faithfully served during all that time. He took care of Elijah's personal needs just as a servant would be expected to do. From what we know about Elijah in Scripture, he was pretty much a loner—a tough guy who wore camel's hair and a leather belt. I can just imagine what serving him must have been like. Likely, there were times when Elisha thought about the affluent family he had left behind, but he stayed with it.

Eventually, the day came when God revealed to his prophets that he would be taking Elijah. Knowing God was about to take him away, Elijah turned to his servant Elisha and asked what he could do for him. The young prophet replied, "Please, let a double portion of your spirit be upon me" (2 Kings 2:9 NASB). Remember, that was the reason Elisha became Elijah's servant in the first place. His time had come, or had it? Elijah's answer: "You have asked a hard thing. *Nevertheless*, if you see me when I am taken from you, it shall be so for you; but if not, it shall not be *so*" (2 Kings 2:10 NASB). Elisha had to remain faithful and continue doing what he had been doing if he was to receive the reward.

## The Reward

What does all of this have to do with us and reigniting our flames? The reward for faithfully serving others with the right heart is a greater measure of the Holy Spirit and his blessing in our lives. It's how the kingdom of God works. Some other biblical examples include Cornelius, a Gentile centurion who served the poor and received the baptism of the Holy Spirit when Peter came to his house (Acts 10); Ruth, a foreigner and young Moabite widow who served her mother-in-law, married a wealthy landowner, and bore a son in the lineage of Christ (Ruth 1–4); David, who faithfully served King Saul, the man who tried to kill him multiple times, and then became king over Israel and God's people (1 Sam. 18; 2 Sam. 5). God rewards faithful service to others when service is given with the right heart (love).

## Pastor Matt

The principle doesn't just apply to those we read about in the Bible. My own pastor is an example of this. Pastor Matt grew up in the church. He and my son Aaron were buddies when they were kids. After college, Matt taught and coached at a local Christian school while serving as youth pastor at our church. For years, he served faithfully and with the right heart—not just for our youth, but also for our senior pastor, Jim. Was his heart "right" every minute of that time? Probably not, but just because he's human.

For several years, whatever pastor Jim needed, Matt took care of without hesitation or complaint. He worked his job at school; took care of his family of four; managed all the youth activities (including mission trips); and was on call for the pastor to do counseling, occasionally preach the Sunday service, and manage many other pastoral duties as they arose. I know it must have been a difficult time for him, but pastor Matt served our senior pastor faithfully, receiving instruction, correction, and wisdom, just as Elisha did in his service to Elijah. Matt didn't get a lot of recognition, and to most, he was "just the youth pastor."

167

## The Mantle Falls on Faithfulness

Having sat under our former pastor for more than thirty years, I can attest to the fact that pastor Jim was and still is a man of prayer, filled with godly wisdom and the Holy Spirit. He founded our church and while it grew in numbers, more importantly, it grew in spiritual depth and maturity. Pastor Jim poured guidance into Matt, imparting a love for people and a heart for the nations into his young protégé and our congregation. Over the years, our church raised up and sent out numerous long- and short-term missionaries from our own number (of which I am one), and supported many others around the world.

Trinity Church was saddened to see pastor Jim retire, but when he did, guess where his mantle fell? It fell squarely on Matt's shoulders. Matt stepped into the position of senior pastor, and I believe a significant portion of the spirit that was in pastor Jim came with him. The pastoral transition was smooth as silk, and left a fresh infusion of the Holy Spirit in the congregation.

When our flame is burning low, service is the last thing we want to do. But in God's economy, that's when it has even greater value. When we serve others, we are in essence denying ourselves, taking up our cross, and following Jesus. I don't know how it happens, but our faith is rekindled.

When a follower of Christ is faithful to serve others with the right heart, even though he or she may or may not feel like it, the Holy Spirit will be manifested in his or her life. Remember, Elijah told Elisha he would receive what he asked for (a double portion of the Spirit that was on Elijah) only if he was there when God took him. Therefore, Elisha never left Elijah's side.

Today, we don't have to attach ourselves to an Elijah to receive the benefit of serving others in love. If we are a believer in Jesus,

the Holy Spirit is already in us. We don't even need to go out looking for people to serve. We just have to be faithful whenever God
brings people and circumstances across our path. That might mean
taking the time to listen to the guy sitting next to you at the doctor's office, or sticking with the commitment you've made to teach
Sunday school. Service isn't always mission work; sometimes it's
mowing a neighbor's yard. Regardless of what service God might
be asking you to do, the most important thing is that it be done in
love, with the right heart.

Elisha was standing right there at Elijah's side when the char-
iot of fire swooped down and snatched up his master. The mantle
fell and he picked it up. As a result of his faithful service, Elisha
received a double portion of the Holy Spirit that was on Elijah.
Already respected as a man of God and a prophet, everyone knew
Elisha was Elijah's successor.

## Washing Hands

During Elisha's time as prophet in the land, an incident happened
where the idolatrous king of Israel, Jehoram, formed an alliance
with the godly king of Judah, Jehoshaphat, along with another
king to fight against Moab (2 Kings 3). After seven days of march-
ing a "roundabout" route without direction or water for the men
or the animals, the three kings were about to give up hope. King
Jehoshaphat finally decided it was time to ask for directions. He
asked, "Is there no prophet of the LORD with us? If there is, we can
ask the LORD what to do through him" (2 Kings 3:11 NLT). Then one
of the servants told them that Elisha was there, and mentioned that
Elisha had poured water on Elijah's hand. And Jehoshaphat said,
"The word of the LORD is with him" (2 Kings 3:12 KJV).

Did you catch that? Elisha could have just as easily been identified as Elijah's successor who received a double portion of God's Spirit, or as the prophet who received Elijah's mantle. But no, Elisha was first recognized as having been a servant, and then as a prophet of the Lord. Pouring water over one's hands was a menial servant's task, but Elisha's faithfulness carried much value in God's economy.

That passage jumped out at me because on my first mission trip to Africa, a young Ugandan girl in my host family's home poured water over my hands, just as they'd done in Elisha's day. She took the cup and tenderly poured water over my hands. She handed me the soap, and after I washed, she poured the water over my hands to rinse them. We never spoke because we didn't speak each other's languages, but love was communicated through her service and our exchanged smiles. I would never dream of asking someone to tend to me in such a personal way, but there in Uganda, this young girl cheerfully served me.

Because he was identified as a servant first, Elisha's heart in serving Elijah was no secret to the people of Israel and Judah. And Jehoshaphat's response, "The word of the LORD is with him," testifies to the spiritual reward for his heart of faithful service.

The mantle of the Holy Spirit is also our reward for serving God. Just as the John Wesley quote says at the beginning of this chapter, we serve God when we serve others in love. Spiritual flames can be rekindled through faithful service if we choose to trust in God and not give up. Jesus told a parable in Matthew 4 about the kingdom of God. He said,

> It is like a mustard seed which, when it is sown on the
> ground, is smaller than all the seeds on earth; but when

it is sown, it grows up and becomes greater than all herbs, and shoots out large branches, so that the birds of the air may nest under its shade. (Mark 4:31–32 NKJV)

It doesn't make sense that something so great would come of something so little, but that's the way it works in God's kingdom. Faith sown in service to others multiplies like that tiny mustard seed. That's how it worked for Elisha, Ruth, David, Esther, Cornelius, and pastor Matt, and that is how it will work for us.

### Note

[1]*Merriam-Webster Dictionary,* online edition, s.v. "servant."

Chapter 15

# The King Is Coming!

"Now learn a lesson from the fig tree."

—Matthew 24:32 ISV

**Maybe because I grew up** in the desert Southwest where one season looks just like the other, Arkansas springtime leaves me with a deep sense of awe when the gray, dead-looking trees begin to show signs of life again. It's as if those buds sprout out promises of good things to come. At the first hint of warm weather, my thoughts turn to shedding all the winter jackets, planting spring flowers, and eating fresh veggies from the garden. There's just nothing better than biting into a vine-ripened tomato doused with salt and pepper!

Ever since Noah emerged from the ark, God promised to keep the cycle of seasons going as long as the earth remains—planting and harvest, cold and heat, summer and winter, day and night. You can count on it. You can always count on God keeping his word.

Fig trees fall into that same sense of expectation. Remember Jesus's disappointment when he looked for figs on a tree and didn't find any? It didn't end well for that particular fig tree. But the cycle of springtime and harvest is one of those things we know will happen. Jesus even used it in Matthew 24 as an illustration of how we can know when he will return. He listed several things that will take place before his return, and then said: "when you see all these things, you know that [God] is near . . ." (Matt. 24:33 ESV). Just as God kept his word about springtime and harvest, he will keep his word about returning for his church.

## Will He Find Faith on the Earth?

What does this have to do with me trying to fan my smoldering embers back into a flame? Because Jesus asked a simple question that we should be asking ourselves: "When the Son of Man comes, will he find faith on earth?" (Luke 18:8 ESV). Will he find it in me? Will I have the kind of faith Jesus is expecting to find in one of his followers?

We believe in God. We love God. But are we ready for God? When the shout goes out that the bridegroom has come for his bride, will we be found waiting with lamps trimmed, full of oil, and burning brightly?

## Jesus at the Door

In Matthew 24, Jesus mentioned that the last days would be filled with deception, wars, rumors of wars, earthquakes, floods, and love growing cold. Clearly all of these fit our times. The problem for us, though, is that we aren't very good at waiting. And we're not very good at believing if we can't see it, prove it, or figure it out for ourselves. We're like the disciple, Thomas; we've been there and done that in our walk with Jesus. When it comes right down to actually *believing* he will do what he says, we'd like a little more proof.

Can't you just hear Thomas's cynicism when the other disciples told him Jesus was alive? "Jesus alive, you say? I'll believe it when I put my fingers in the holes where the nails were driven into his hands and touch his side where the sword drew out water and blood. Jesus is dead. I saw him take his last breath, and I was there when they took his bloody body down from the cross and laid it in the tomb. I need more proof."

We believe God and his promise in Genesis 8 to continue the cycle of seasons—springtime and harvest, winter and summer, and so on—because we see it happen every year. I believe that in the spring the weather will warm up and all the dead-looking trees will begin to bud. I believe that the sprouting buds will turn into green leaves and that the trees will bear fruit in the summer. I also fully believe that after a few months, the weather will turn cooler again and the leaves will change color and fall to the ground. And finally, I believe it will get cold enough for me to dig out my winter jacket and boots when the trees look dry and dead again. We know the cycle will start all over again, because the changing seasons are God's promise, and he does what he says he will do.

## The First Coming of Christ

Believing God regarding the things we can see is easy, but what about the promises that aren't so easy to track? Think about what it must have been like for the Jewish people under Roman rule a few thousand years ago. The Scriptures were full of promises for a Savior, but it had been a long time since any prophets brought God's Word to the people. Even though the signs were there for the prophesies of a Messiah or Savior to be fulfilled, not many were expecting it to happen. They were consumed with life, work, and family, and were existing under an oppressive ruling government, just living out their day-to-day lives.

But as life continued as usual for everyone else in Israel, an angel paid an unexpected visit to a young Jewish girl in Nazareth. He told her she was chosen to carry God incarnate in her womb— the Messiah and Savior for the entire world, for all time. Mary didn't ask for proof, she just asked how it could happen since she was a virgin. After the angel explained that the Holy Spirit would come upon her and she would conceive the Son of God, she believed him and said, "Let it happen to me as you have said" (Luke 1:38 NLV). Wow! And just like that, prophecy was fulfilled.

Nothing on the outside looked any different. The Romans were still in charge, and life went on as usual. Mary had to face the scorn of her betrothed husband, and she risked rejection because of what appeared to be a promiscuous act. Even so, Jesus was born and grew up just like everyone else.

The signs were all there, but no one was paying attention. Then, when Jesus was thirty years old, his time had come. His cousin, John the Baptist, baptized him and the world changed. We all know the amazing miracles and teachings of Jesus, but it was the fact that he was God come to the earth to save mankind from sin that changed the world. His life, death, and resurrection fulfilled more than 350 prophecies from Genesis to Malachi—everything from his birthplace to the betrayal to the Crucifixion and more.

Think about this: out of all the cities and scores of nations in existence all over the world, Micah named Bethlehem of Judea as the birthplace of the Messiah seven hundred years before he was born! (Mic. 5:2). Isaiah said he would be born of a virgin, and he was (Isa. 7:14). And in 1012 BC, the prophet Zechariah specified that the Messiah's hands and feet would be pierced—a clear reference to death by crucifixion—eight hundred years before the Romans even instituted crucifixion as a form of capital punishment! (Zech. 12:10). Another reference and prophecy depicting the Crucifixion is in Psalms as well—a different writer in a different century (Ps. 22:16).

The signs of the times were all there. God said he would send the Messiah into the world, and he did. As remarkable as all of this is, God's people, for the most part, were oblivious, cynical, and even hostile toward Jesus and his followers.

## History Repeated

Jesus said he was coming back for his bride, the church (that's you and me), and he is right at the door. God doesn't change—all his words are fulfilled, without exception. In other words, he still does what he says he will do—today! We can count on it. He said he would send a Messiah, and he did, exactly as he said he would.

The fig tree is bursting forth with buds and leaves, and for the most part, God's people are just as oblivious, cynical, and hostile as they were the first time Jesus came on the scene. Peter, a Galilean fisherman and Jesus's disciple, inspired and empowered by the Holy Spirit, prophesied and wrote this about the people who would be living in the days prior to the Second Coming of Christ:

> Most importantly, I want to remind you that in the last days scoffers will come, mocking the truth and following their own desires. They will say, "What happened to the promise that Jesus is coming again? From before the times of our ancestors, everything has remained the same since the world was first created." They deliberately forget that God made the heavens long ago by the word

of his command, and he brought the earth out from the water and surrounded it with water. Then he used the water to destroy the ancient world with a mighty flood. And by the same word, the present heavens and earth have been stored up for fire. They are being kept for the day of judgment, when ungodly people will be destroyed. (2 Pet. 3:3–7 NLT)

In a letter he wrote to Timothy, the great apostle Paul gave insight and warning about the last days—if this doesn't describe the world we live in now, I don't know what does.

You should know this, Timothy, that in the last days there will be very difficult times. For people will love only themselves and their money. They will be boastful and proud, scoffing at God, disobedient to their parents, and ungrateful. They will consider nothing sacred. They will be unloving and unforgiving; they will slander others and have no self-control. They will be cruel and hate what is good. They will betray their friends, be reckless, be puffed up with pride, and love pleasure rather than God. They will act religious, but they will reject the power that could make them godly. (2 Tim. 3:1–5 NLT)

Here we are in the twenty-first century, and much of the church is busy doing superficial churchy activities, being careful not to offend anyone for fear of losing members. We embrace the loving heart of God while rejecting his holiness, righteousness, and judgment over sin. Seldom, if ever, do I hear the word "repent" from the pulpit.

Divorce and infidelity statistics within the church mirror those in the secular world. A huge portion of the church looks no different—outwardly, inwardly, or spiritually—from the world. Is it any wonder we have lost our first love and our flames are burning low? Christianity for many people in the twenty-first century has devolved to a "bless me" club, looking for God to give us everything and anything we want without any conviction to surrender our will and our lives to the one who gave his life for us.

We read Scriptures about the Second Coming of Christ, pay attention to news reports, read books and articles, and listen to televangelists believing that, yes, Jesus could come at any time. But then we go on with life as usual. We know he's coming, but our priorities and focus are in the wrong place.

## Focus

I'll never forget the time my husband and I invited our pastor and his wife for dinner. To some, this probably wouldn't be a big deal; but because I am a perfectionist by nature, everything, of course, had to be perfect.

Being somewhat of a "foodie," I pride myself on being a fairly decent cook. I thought about making a great gourmet meal, but because I wasn't sure what foods the pastor and his wife would like, I decided to play it safe and make a roast beef dinner. I figured most people like beef, and the meal would be easy to prepare.

My pastor and his wife had never been to our home, so I pulled out all the stops. To keep from rushing around trying to get ready at the last minute, I laid out my clothes early. On the day they were to come, I spent the day cleaning house. Wanting to make a good impression, I attacked every corner of the house with militant fervor. Every speck of dust that had comfortably resided in nooks and crannies for months was forcibly removed. When I finally put away my vacuum cleaner, cleaning rags, and Windex, the house smelled great and was officially cleaned and ready for my pastor and his wife. But dinner wasn't.

I'd been so busy cleaning, I lost sight of the purpose of his visit. Because my focus was on making a good impression, my cleaning spree didn't end until about an hour before the pastor was to arrive—and I hadn't even taken the roast out of the refrigerator. Anyone who knows anything about cooking a roast knows a four-pound roast has to slow-cook for hours if one wants it to be fall-apart tender. I made an impression on the pastor—it just wasn't the one I was looking for. I knew he was coming, but was unprepared in the way that truly mattered.

Jesus is coming soon. The signs of the times are all around us, but our attention is focused on the wrong things, and our flames are burning dangerously low in the process. Churches are filled with people who embrace a loving, merciful God—he is loving and merciful—but they are living, unashamedly and without conviction, in unforgiveness, fornication, and other sins. If Jesus is coming for a bride who is "without a spot or wrinkle" (Eph. 5:27 NLT), we had better get our laundry done before God does it for us. "But who can endure the day of his coming? Who can stand when he appears? For he will be like a refiner's fire or a launderer's soap" (Mal. 3:2 NIV).

When Isaiah the prophet found himself in the presence of God, he fell on his face and cried out, "Woe to me! . . . I am ruined! For I am a man of unclean lips, and I live among a people of unclean lips, and my eyes have seen the King, the LORD Almighty" (Isa. 6:5 NIV). And Isaiah was a prophet!

As I wrote earlier, Jesus is coming for a bride without spot or wrinkle. His appearing will be sooner than we expect—all the signs are there. I don't know about you, but I want to be ready when that day arrives. It is my prayer that your faith has been reignited and fanned back into a flame after setting your heart on this pilgrimage to the heart of God.

# Chapter 16

# Here We Are

"And now here we are,
standing inside your gates, O Jerusalem.
Jerusalem is a well-built city;
its seamless walls cannot be breached.
All the tribes of Israel—the LORD's people—
make their pilgrimage here."

—Psalms 122:2–4 (NLT)

"**Are we there yet?**" **How** many times have I heard *that* question echo from the back seat of a car on a long road trip? Probably thousands. But guess what? We made it! Here we are! Though our pursuit of a closer, more faith-filled walk with God will never be over until we meet Jesus face-to-face, this pilgrimage we've traveled together is drawing to a close—and here we are, standing within his gates.

I hope you've made a few new discoveries, in addition to rediscovering some forgotten or lost truths from the Scriptures that have helped you fan your spiritual flame and reignite your faith in

God. Like it says in Romans, "For in the gospel the righteousness of God is revealed—a righteousness that is by faith from first to last, just as it is written: 'The righteous will live by faith'" (Rom. 1:17 NIV). God's righteousness and truths are uncovered and revealed from one faith experience to the next. Igniting our faith is a journey and a process—a pilgrimage. It's amazing what the Holy Spirit will do in us once we make the commitment and take the first step in seeking him. We've covered a lot of ground on this journey in a very short time. It reminds me of a whirlwind road trip to California I made last year.

## Road Trip

Last year I got a really crazy idea. I wanted to bring my eighty-three-year-old dad, who lives in California, to Arkansas to spend the Thanksgiving and Christmas holidays with my family. Of course, my crazy idea wasn't bringing him here—it was *how* I wanted to bring him. I could have flown him, but that's what a sane person would do, right?

I got a little sentimental one day, thinking back on my "army brat" childhood. I have such fond memories of how much fun my brothers and I had when Dad took us on road trips across the states after receiving his military orders to move. So I thought, wouldn't it be fun to take a couple of my grandkids on a road trip to pick up Grandpa and bring him back to Arkansas? Dad always stopped and took in the historical sights. Because he was a schoolteacher before he went into the Army, he taught us everything from how to read a map to how to recognize different types of mountains and plateaus as we traveled across the states. The unfolding geography outside our car window was our schoolroom. I wanted to give Luke, fourteen, and Farran, eleven, the same kind of experience.

Because they are both homeschooled, they could bring their work along and we could turn it into a big three-thousand-mile field trip. From start to finish, we would have eleven days. If I planned it right, we'd have just enough time to see a few sights, pick up Grandpa, and get home before Thanksgiving. I talked to my kids and grandkids, and even though it was a crazy idea, everyone was on board. So with plenty of snacks loaded for the road, we set off on our adventure.

I had a GPS, but picked up an old-school paper road atlas to teach Luke and Farran how to read a map and navigate road signs. Every day, the kids had to write down two things they learned the day before. We had a blast. The trip was a fun learning experience.

On the way to California, they learned about Route 66 along Interstate 40, the Trail of Tears in Oklahoma, old missions in New Mexico, American Indian reservations in Arizona, and volcanic rock in the California desert. After we got to Grandpa's house, we took a day and visited the Pacific Ocean and fought Los Angeles traffic to see Hollywood up close and personal. The next day, we packed up the car and started the return trip home with Grandpa.

On the trip home, we spent the night at my brother's house in Las Vegas and took in the neon lights. The old schoolteacher came out in Grandpa when we visited Hoover Dam, and the kids learned a lot about its history. We stopped for lunch at my other brother's home in Kingman, Arizona, and were off to spend the night in Williams, Arizona. The next morning, we rode the train to see the Grand Canyon, the highlight of the trip.

I discovered that my father, who had lived in that part of the country most of his life, had never taken the time to go there. This was his first time to see the phenomenal beauty of the Grand Canyon. The next day, we drove across the desert and took in the

Cadillac Ranch on Interstate 40. Our last stop before home was at the huge cross in Groom, Texas. Below the cross are several life-sized, chillingly lifelike bronze sculptures depicting Jesus's Crucifixion—amazing! When our journey ended, none of us were the same.

## Pilgrimage Parallels and Paradigms

Sometimes real life parallels or even intersects with our spiritual life. In fact, as we made our way through the pages of this book on our spiritual pilgrimage, I couldn't help but think about the spiritual parallels from my crazy road trip across the desert. On both the physical road trip and this pilgrimage to fanning our flame, there were obstacles to overcome, new discoveries to be made, and lessons to learn. The dryness we started out with at the Trail of Tears ended at the cross with renewed and reignited faith in God.

On this journey, I pray that we've each discovered new things that maybe weren't new—just new to us. Like Farran putting her feet in the ocean or Grandpa seeing the Grand Canyon for the first time, God's Word is eternal. When we take the time to stop and take it in, we are awestruck.

God may have shown you something new and amazing for the first time, and even though you've been walking with the Lord for a while, you've never seen it. Perhaps you're new to the Christian faith, and you were challenged on one of the stops of our pilgrimage to step out and get your feet wet. For myself, I found that rediscovering forgotten treasures along the way strengthened my faith. I needed to rediscover my old, gray chair and the childlike faith I once had. God has also challenged me to dig for diamonds in his Word, and then allow him to cut them into my life.

Some of the stops on our journey were interesting to Farran, but not to Luke, and vice versa. I think the same is true for us here; you may not have been wounded in the church, but needed to unpack a little pride or unforgiveness. None of us are perfect. We all have flaws and failures, but we also all have Jesus. And we can do all things through Christ who strengthens us. That's why we started this pilgrimage in the first place—to be strengthened in our faith.

## Three Required Pilgrimages

Our spiritual journey can be compared to the pilgrimage God instructed his children to take three times a year to celebrate three important festivals (Deut. 16:16). Their pilgrimages took them to the temple in Jerusalem, where the presence of God resided. All along the way, the travelers sang the Song of Ascents, Psalms 120–134. With each step, God's people drew closer to the temple and to spiritual communion with him.

I found it interesting that God *required* this journey, not just once in a lifetime or even once a year, but three times every year! The pilgrimages were a continual reminder of their relationship to their God. Hmm. We may not need to pack our bags and set out on a physical journey to Jerusalem three times a year, but it makes sense to take note of how important this pilgrimage was to God, since we've been on our own pilgrimages to seek him and his fire. God obviously saw their need for spiritual renewal, and we are no different.

What were the three required pilgrimages these ancient Israelites made? The first was the Festival of Unleavened Bread, celebrating their delivery from bondage in Egypt. The second was Shavuot, the Festival of Weeks, remembering the giving of the Torah (God's Word) exactly seven weeks after the Exodus and Passover. It is also known as Pentecost. The third festival was Sukkot, the Festival of Tabernacles, which celebrates the wandering of the Israelites in the desert for forty years, when they had to rely only upon God for direction, sustenance, and protection.

## Salvation, God's Word, Dependence

I don't claim to be a biblical scholar, but God does reveal his Word and mysteries to simple-minded people like me. When I look at these three feasts, I cannot help but find a parallel in the Jewish pilgrimages and the important pilgrimages a Christian believer must take in their walk with God—salvation, the gift of God's Word and the Holy Spirit, and total dependency on God.

Our first pilgrimage is a return to our first love. The Israelites made the journey to the temple to remember when and how God delivered them from bondage in Egypt—Passover. Our Passover is our deliverance from the bondage of sin. Some of us have not-so-pretty pasts. We weren't always good church people—or, maybe you were. But at some point, you were confronted by your own sin and separation from God. The mirror of God's Word reveals that we all have fallen short of the only standard that matters (Rom. 3:23). We all need a Savior. We came to God through faith in Jesus Christ, the Passover lamb, who not only spilled his blood on the cross, but suffered one of the most horrific forms of torturous deaths ever devised by man. When Jesus was resurrected on the third day after his death, his sacrifice ultimately purchased the victory over sin and death for each one of us who believe. We *must* return to our first love.

The second Jewish pilgrimage feast was Shavuot, or what we call Pentecost. In the feast of Shavuot, God's people remember when he gave his Word, or law, to guide his people into all truth. They had God's Word, but didn't believe it.

There is an interesting verse in the book of Hebrews referring to the Word of God given to the Jewish people on their Exodus from Egypt and their unbelief. Hebrews 4:2 says: "For indeed we have had good news preached to us, just as they also; but the word they heard did not profit them, because it was not united by faith in those who heard" (NASB). The writer of Hebrews drew a parallel between these ancient Jews and us who have the New Testament gospel. Having the Word of God alone wasn't enough for them, and it isn't enough for us either. It must be accompanied by faith. The Word of God must be quickened in us—made alive. That happens through the Holy Spirit—Pentecost, the second pilgrimage.

Just before he ascended, Jesus instructed his disciples to go to Jerusalem and wait for the promise of the Father. He said, "But you shall receive power when the Holy Spirit has come upon you; and you shall be witnesses to Me in Jerusalem, and in all Judea and Samaria, and to the end of the earth" (Acts 1:8 NKJV). We can do nothing without the power and guidance of the Holy Spirit, so this Pentecost pilgrimage is critical to our faith walk and spiritual flame.

The third pilgrimage to Jerusalem was for the feast of Sukkot, when the Hebrew travelers remembered their total reliance upon God—remembering *and* rejoicing in God's provision and care for them during those forty long years of wandering in the desert (Deut. 16:14–15).

Can you imagine living on a daily miracle from God as you gathered up sweet manna every morning? Or never having to worry about new shoes because your old ones didn't wear out—for forty years? It is important that we too look back and remember all the ways God has cared for, guided, and protected us, even in our rebellion and unbelief. It is a testimony to God's unfailing love and mercy.

We can do all things through Christ who strengthens us, but we can do nothing apart from him. In this pilgrimage, we are reminded that all things come from God. Our own righteousness is like filthy rags. Interestingly, this third pilgrimage festival immediately follows the Days of Awe and Repentance. Sukkot represents a time of restored fellowship with the Lord—his dwelling among his redeemed people.

In the final steps of our pilgrimage to reignite our faith in God, hold in your mind and heart these three focal points of the festival pilgrimages, and how we as believers also must keep them as the focus of our own.

- Passover—Returning to our first love and remembering our salvation by the precious shed blood of our Savior, Jesus Christ. Our every sin wiped away for all eternity.
- Pentecost—Resolving to wait on and trust in the power of the Holy Spirit, who quickens his Word and enables us to become witnesses to Jesus Christ, guiding us into all truth wherever we go or whomever we meet in the world.
- Sukkot—The feast that follows repentance. Returning to a total dependence on God for strength, wisdom, guidance, and sustenance—a restored fellowship and faith in our God.

As we have journeyed together on this pilgrimage to strengthen our faith, we've trimmed away some of the charred places in our wicks and replenished our oil supply. My prayer is that with our lamps burning a little brighter on the path in front of us, our steps will be surer and our faith will be more confident in God, our Savior.